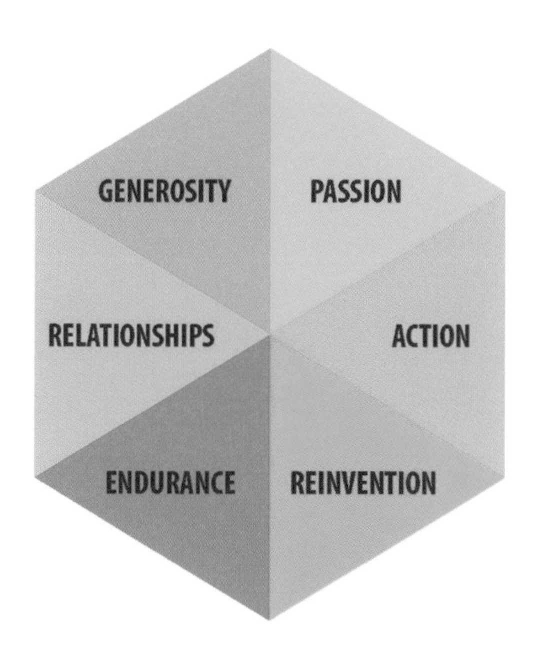

THE WISDOM WAY

Six Guiding Principles for Longevity and Success

Passion

Action

Reinvention

Endurance

Relationships

Generosity

The WISDOM Way

by

TOM ROLANDO

PORTLAND • OREGON

Cover and interior design by Masha Shubin

Images unless otherwise noted © Wisdom Adhesives.
Cover image: *The Giant's Causeway* © Jim Richardson, National Geographic Collection, used with permission. *Butch Cassidy and the Sundance Kid* used with permission from Inmagine. Laurel leaves © Microvector; Bigstockphoto.com. Vecor ribbon © Adroach; Bigstockphoto.com

Publisher: Inkwater Press | www.inkwaterpress.com

ISBN-13 978-1-62901-145-5 | ISBN-10 1-62901-145-2

Printed in the U.S.A.
All paper is acid free and meets all ANSI standards for archival quality paper.

3 5 7 9 10 8 6 4 2

This book is dedicated to Phillip Wisdom, founder of Wisdom Adhesives, and the thousands of customers whom Wisdom Adhesives has had the privilege to service throughout its 140 years.

We look forward to the next 140 years.

A special thank you goes to all of those people who contributed to *The Wisdom Way* book:

Glenn Auerbach

Kevin Callahan

Brett Musnicki

Cathy Westhouse

Jeff Wisdom

&

The Staff at Wisdom Adhesives Worldwide
Past and Present

ABOUT THE COVER

Giant's Causeway

The **Giant's Causeway** is a rock formation found in County Antrim, Northern Ireland, in the nearby of the town of Bushmills. It is believed that these volcanic rocks developed into "naturally" hexagonal shapes when water began to cool them millions of years ago. There are more than 40,000 perfectly shaped, interlocking hexagonally shaped basalt columns that are believed to be the result of ancient volcanic eruptions.

The Giant's Causeway was named as the fourth greatest natural wonder in the United Kingdom. The tops of the columns form stepping stones that lead from the cliff foot and disappear under the sea. Although the vast majority of the columns are hexagonal, there are also some with four-, five-, seven-, and eight-sided columns. The tallest are about 40 feet high, and the solidified lava is up to 100 feet thick in places.

The Giant's Causeway is owned and managed by the National Trust and is the most popular tourist attraction in Northern Ireland.

"The Strength of the Hexagon"

CONTENTS

FOREWORD

By Jeff Wisdom

RUNNING A BUSINESS CAN BE CHALLENGING.

Running a family-held business can be very challenging.

Running a multi-generational family business can be ridiculously challenging.

Operating a fifth generation, family-owned company, where the odds of success are very low—less than 3% of all family-run companies make it to even the third generation—that is now 140 years strong is … well you get the picture.

Family businesses are the best, but can also be the worst, of times. A tremendous amount of responsibility is carried by one who heads up a family business. Working to make it successful, employing family members, and hopefully, passing on a legacy to the next generation are just some of

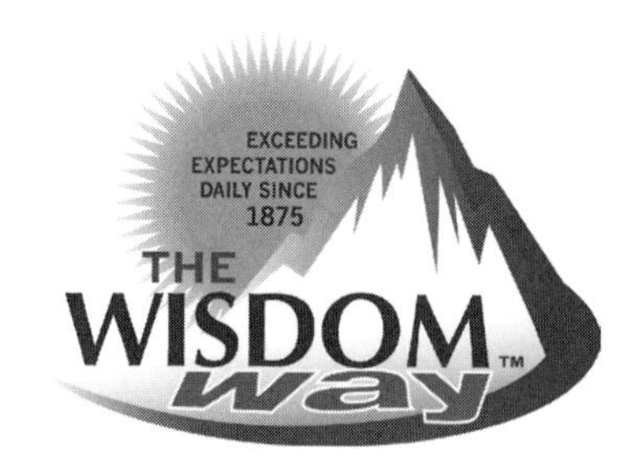

the burdens a family business owner faces every day. Every new day is met with the challenge of figuring out how to keep the company successfully rolling along. Success is tempered by continuously pending future concerns, and failure is often met with gut-wrenching consequences that affect the lives of the people I care about the most, and I wouldn't trade it for anything in the world.

To me, *The Wisdom Way* is an all-encompassing way of doing business, from the types of products we manufacture and sell to the relationships we build with our customers and the way our employees and the communities in which we operate are treated.

Paramount in *The Wisdom Way* is our customers. The customer is the central reason why we are in business. We are not in business to self-serve our wants and needs but to service the customer in the best fashion possible. The fruits of our labors can only be valued once the customer is satisfied. We work hard to ensure our customers are treated with the highest standards of *The Wisdom Way*.

Treat customers how you wish to be treated. It is a very simple concept but one that can readily be lost in the pursuit of doing the best one can.

I am a very blessed and grateful person, as I am fortunate to run a business with so many dedicated people serving those whom make our existence possible—our customers. *The Wisdom Way* is founded on three main components:

- Our Customers
- Our Employees
- The Communities in Which We Operate and Conduct Business

These three entities are vital to our success. Without customers, we have no business. Without employees, we have no one to serve our customers. Without communities, we have no infrastructure from which to operate.

Wisdom Adhesives Worldwide is a privately held company headquartered just outside of Chicago, Illinois, and established in 1875. I am the fifth generation owner of the company. Wisdom Adhesives is a manufacturer of specialty leading-edge, environmentally compatible, water-based and hot melt adhesives used in the packaging, converting, product assembly, and graphic arts industries. Through my now long-lasting career, there have been many ups and downs and many times when there seemed to be no light at the end of the tunnel. Still, we pressed on, knowing that sticking to key core principles would carry us through any hardships. Early on, I decided to make a list of key attributes needed to survive and thrive in the business world:

- Passion
- Action
- Reinvention
- Endurance
- Relationships
- Generosity

The number six represents the strongest of all chemical structures, the hexagon ring. The six guiding principles were and are the key to Wisdom's 140+ years of operation and service to its customers, employees, and communities.

While the vast majority of the actions supporting *The Wisdom Way* are of the best regards, it has not been the smoothest of roads. Some might say it took four generations and a 125+ years to get it right.

I've learned to apply the six principles on a daily basis in both my personal and professional life, be it with simple problem solving or in dealing with the most complex of issues. I've also used the six principles to guide our company thinking and long-term planning. In doing so, we've been able to define a culture that prides itself on Passion, Action, Reinvention, Endurance, Relationships, and Generosity.

Passion has always driven the company. Come to Wisdom Adhesives Worldwide and you will see Passion in all our efforts. Action is the guiding principle of the company. When there is a job to be done, Action will be taken. Wisdom Adhesive's quick response time in getting to the customer with answers is legendary. One of the key principles of *The Wisdom Way* is the ability to adapt to and to Reinvent the organization to fit the ever-changing environment. This is where it begins and ends for many of us. Are we willing to adapt to changing climates or are we merely going to do what we've always done? Once we've committed to change, the path of *The Wisdom Way* can begin, and it will take a multitude of dimensions to accomplish it.

With Passion, Action, and Reinvention comes Endurance. Passion will fuel the Action and allow for constant Reinvention, but it takes Endurance to be successful over the long haul. To have Endurance you need the best of teams. Teams ranging from customers to employees to vendors are all imperative to the success or failure of the business, and having those Relationships working in top order is paramount. The generations before me have taught me to be a team player with the best Relationships possible, to be grateful for what I have, and not to assume tomorrow, as it is not promised to any of us. The last and final principle, Generosity, is the payback to those that need it the most—the strength of *The Wisdom Way.*

Wisdom Adhesives Worldwide has a long history and is now in its 140th year of continuous operations, making it the oldest and longest running company of its kind in North America and possibly the world. There are very few companies that can say they are 140 years old but have actually only come of age in the past decade. But as all business owners know, it's not about what you've done in the past, but rather what you will do in the future. We believe our future is bright and look forward to the next generations and the next 140 years.

Before diving into the guiding principles, a history lesson is in order, and a Brief, Long History will follow. Yet this book is not about the specifics of Wisdom Adhesives Worldwide; it is about the specifics of *The Wisdom Way* and its guiding principles.

From humble beginnings and through depressions, recessions, and wars, the company has not only survived, it has flourished. Each of *The Wisdom Way* principles has been learned and repeated over the life of the company's existence, and only now is it in print for all to know. *The Wisdom Way* dives into each of these principles to help the reader understand the path of Wisdom Adhesives Worldwide. I truly believe one can readily apply the six principles to any business or any endeavor and be successful. We've done it, now it is your turn.

The Wisdom Way path is rewarding for all who truly embrace it. Pursue business interests and life to the fullest and enjoy your read of *The Wisdom Way* and use it to find your path to success.

PREFACE

CHEMISTRY CAN BE A CONFUSING SUBJECT TO those unfamiliar with all its scientific nomenclature and formulas. It is much like learning a language, albeit a technical one. As science tends to be, it is a field that affects us all, whether we are aware of its workings or not. Chemicals and chemistry are all around us. Chemistry stands to help us understand the composition and structure of all things physical and the properties and change of matter. However, it is also full of analogies applicable to everyday life.

In nature, the single strongest chemical structure is the hexagon. The hexagon is an entirely symmetrical shape, having six congruent sides as well as six congruent internal angles. The hexagon can be tiled seamlessly and infinitely, and because of its circular shape, it can do so in the most economical formation. As the hexagon is a source of strength in nature, it is also the foundation of *The Wisdom Way*. Each

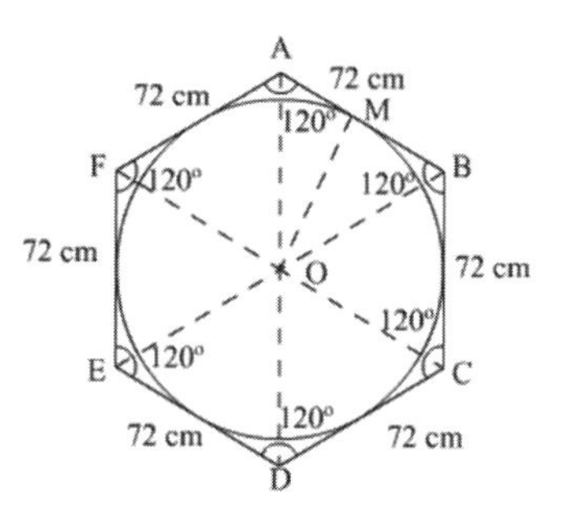

side is equally important, but it is the whole from which the strength is drawn.

Bees are no stranger to the wonders of this perfectly symmetrical brick and mortar. A beehive is made entirely of hexagonal tiling and stands to hold over 20 times its own weight. Bees have no rulers or protractors and, as far as we can tell, do not study geometry in depth. It is through necessity that they have found this unique shape for creating their structure. In the same way, Wisdom Adhesives Worldwide has come to understand our own composition and how it has led to our success through the decades.

To demonstrate further another beneficiary of the hexagon's strength, look to the composition and geometric design of graphite. Graphite is a unique element composed of a molecular honeycomb. Graphite may not have the strength of diamond, but what it lacks in strength, it makes up in efficacy. Much like adhesives, graphite is used in an unconnected array of applications. Be it pencil lead, golf club shafts, or airplane wings, graphite draws its utility from its unique combination of high strength, relative light weight, and tremendous flexibility. This is where we find common ground.

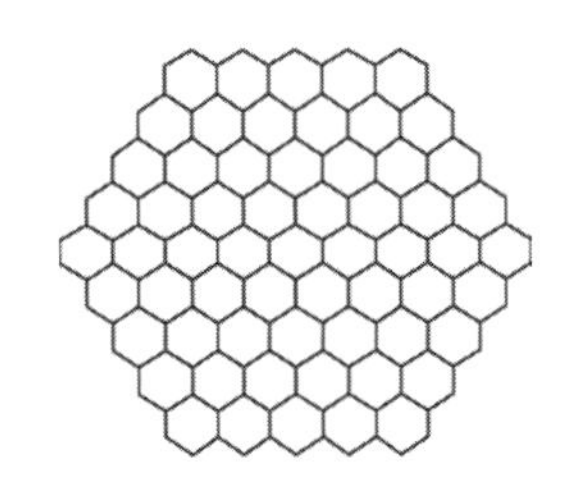

Wisdom Adhesives Worldwide is not so different from graphite. Wisdom Adhesives is versatile, stronger when working in unison, and has the ability to fit the needs of a variety of unique situations. What Wisdom Adhesives has found is that the unique hexagonal structure and teamwork approach has been the primary drive responsible for its success. Wisdom Adhesives has never been an industry giant, nor has it sought to be; instead, it focuses its energy on doing a great job for the customers it has the privilege to serve.

Unlike chemistry, the business world is not a place that adheres to a rigid path or formula. It is an ever-changing landscape that demands constant innovation and transformation to fuel success. This, in turn, is where the complexity and challenge of industry lies. Be it technology, economy, policy, or simply necessity, there is always a variable presenting an opportunity for advancement. Each new opportunity calls for creativity and innovation and a keen understanding of the issues at hand. In this way, chemistry is more kind, as matter performs predictably. Without a solid foundation, a business is likely to be lost or supremely challenged in times of turmoil or distress.

Being around for more than 13 decades, Wisdom Adhesives has seen, adapted to, and become quite familiar with this ever-changing landscape. Not only has Wisdom Adhesives stuck around, which is feat enough, but it has continued to grow nearly each and every year, often at a very high rate. Even when challenged by depression, recession, or legislation, the fiber of the company has not been broken. Wisdom Adhesives Worldwide is not the perfect model company and most certainly has never claimed to be such. Instead, it aims to show how the makeup has paved the road to success, even when the odds have been stacked against it.

Six simple principles, each equal and connected to form the hexagon, make up *The Wisdom Way*.

THE WISDOM WAY

A BRIEF, LONG HISTORY OF WISDOM ADHESIVES WORLDWIDE

Wisdom Adhesives Worldwide is the longest running adhesive manufacturer in North America and possibly the world, celebrating 140 years in business.

Phillip Wisdom, Founder of Wisdom and Co.

Wisdom Adhesives' five generations of family ownership have created a thriving professional culture with a rich and eventful history.

Phillip Wisdom, the great-great-great-great-grandfather of current CEO Jeff Wisdom, founded Wisdom and Co. in

Wisdom and Co. building on Canal Street in Chicago

the year 1875. The original place of business was located on Canal Street in Chicago, Illinois, and initially sold adhesives to bookbinders and publishers in the aftermath of The Great Chicago Fire. Back in the earliest days of Wisdom's existence, deliveries were made to local customers by horse and carriage.

While the adhesives landscape has changed drastically since the company's conception, Phillip Wisdom laid down a foundation of core values that has withstood the test of time and continues to guide how Wisdom Adhesives operates today. Dedication to Wisdom's customers, employees, and the community remains a commitment that drives how the company operates on a day-to-day basis. A focus on Wisdom's family, which encompasses these three important groups, has been a part of the business philosophy for all five generations of Wisdom's existence.

Since the time of Phillip Wisdom, Wisdom Adhesives has experienced tremendous growth and success. In 1925 the company's annual sales reached a milestone level, far outpacing the previous year's sales by a two-fold margin, for the very first time, and essentially, doubling the company. After expanding the operations to locations in Franklin Park, Illinois, and growing the product line to include graphic arts and paper converting adhesive solutions, George Wisdom (second-generation CEO of Wisdom Adhesives) took the helm of the company and modernized Wisdom's sales, establishing accounting and manufacturing processes that were used well into the late 1960s.

By the late 1990s, Wisdom had matured into one of the strongest mid-size industrial adhesive manufacturers in North America. Warehousing and production for Wisdom's products had reached both coasts, with locations on the West Coast and in Northeastern and Southeastern United States. Wisdom's high-quality bookbinding adhesives were also being delivered to international customers in both Europe and Asia.

Despite today's fast-paced, ever-changing and often overwhelming world of business, Wisdom Adhesives has continued to thrive and grow, led by current CEO and fifth-generation family owner Jeff Wisdom. Since Jeff Wisdom has assumed leadership of the company, a revolutionary environmentally-sustainable adhesive line has been established, the WizNet Online Ordering System has been instituted, and Wisdom's operations have expanded to Canada, Mexico, and Asia. Wisdom's success in the current economic environment has been fueled by a continued dedication to the values set forth by founder Phillip Wisdom. Wisdom customers continue to receive innovative and competitive products at fair prices and personalized customer service that is second to none. Wisdom employees enjoy a sustainable workplace with a strong emphasis on family values and work/life balance. The Wisdom Family Foundation has been established to provide financial support for the overall wellbeing of children and families and to give back to the community that has given so much to Wisdom Adhesives.

The history of Wisdom Adhesives reveals the key ingredient to its continued success: relentless innovation combined with proven business principles. The relentless pursuit of innovation to keep up with a changing technological and economic landscape is at the core of Wisdom Adhesives. At the same time, adherence to core a set of proven business principles that help ensure satisfaction and sustainability has always been job number one at Wisdom Adhesives, with maximum focus on customers, employees, and the communities in which business is conducted. It is the belief by all at Wisdom Adhesives that a continuation on this path of innovation and principles is paramount for adapting to business for the next 140 years!

Chronological time line appears on page 145.

THE WISDOM WAY

The *Wisdom Way* is a comprehensive approach to conducting business at Wisdom Adhesives, with regards to three equally important constituents:

- Customers
- Employees
- Communities in which it operates.

The key to *The Wisdom Way* is the emphasis and value placed on the three constituents, leading to the ultimate success and purpose of Wisdom Adhesives.

Customers—Wisdom Adhesives is dedicated to offering environmentally safe, unique, leading-edge, and competitive technologies and products at a fair value to the customers that it serves. Customers have always been number one at Wisdom Adhesives—since 1875.

Several key customer-focused programs include:

- The development, manufacture, and sale of adhesive products with the best technologies with the very best economics

- Environmentally compatible adhesive products such as the GreenBond Sustainable Adhesive, ClearBond, WizAssure, WizBond, and WizBond II product lines

- "Customer is King" Program

- Wisdom Total Quality Management (WTQM), with Lean Six Sigma Focused Accelerated Service Teams (LSS-FAST)

Employees—Wisdom Adhesives is dedicated to maintaining a sustainable work environment for all employees, with a strong emphasis on family values and work/life balance. All employees are encouraged to reach their full potential in a highly ethical and appreciative work environment. Programs include:

- Efficient Compact Organization—ECO^2
- Wisdom World Awards
- Stakeholder Program
- Incubator Program
- Mentor Program

Communities—Wisdom Adhesives is a strong advocate of shaping and enhancing environmental and public policy in the communities in which operates. Wisdom Adhesives donates a defined percentage of its pre-tax profits, mainly through the Wisdom Foundation, to qualified entities—many with a sustainable environmental focus. Programs include:

- The Wisdom Foundation
- Sustainable product lines
- Environmental impact analysis
- Green manufacturing practices

There is a creed at Wisdom Adhesives to recognize the manner in which *The Wisdom Way* is emphasized and it is shown on the next page.

THE WISDOM CUSTOMER CREED

WILLINGNESS TO "THINK OUTSIDE THE BOX." In today's adhesives market, many manufacturers are setting the "rules to play by." Wisdom Adhesives is the exception.

IDEALISTIC IS OUR NATURE AT WISDOM ADHESIVES and it is how we respond to customers.

SERVICE, SERVICE, AND MORE SERVICE IS THE motto at Wisdom Adhesives—resulting in overall savings to the customer.

DEMONSTRATE CONTINUAL NEW AND CUSTOMized product development.

ON CALL, ONLINE, ON SITE, AND ON TIME, ALL part of the Wisdom Adhesives complete service package focusing on the customer.

MEETING AND EXCEEDING CUSTOMER REQUIREments since 1875. That's 140 years!

In many ways, *The Wisdom Way* is about getting it done. Use of the six principles only enhances the getting it done!

Consider the manufacturing giant Nike and its slogan "Just Do It." This exemplifies *The Wisdom Way.*

Apart from its application to the world of sports, these three simple words are very relevant in today's marketplace and, specifically, important in describing how Wisdom Adhesives operates.

Getting it done is what it is all about. It separates the wannabes from the achievers and failure from success. At Wisdom Adhesives, "getting it done" always includes:

- Serving the customer. It's a core Wisdom Way constituent.

- Persevering when others are telling you a task is impossible. That takes Passion, Action, Reinvention, Endurance, Relationships, and Generosity—in short, all of *The Wisdom Way* principles.

- Finishing the task and not pointing to oneself as if you scored a touchdown or made a game-saving tackle. Heck, in today's athletic world, making a routine play is often followed by pointing to oneself and asking the crowd to cheer for nothing more than doing your job.

- Cutting through the red tape and completing the job.

- Closing the sale.

- Ensuring the sale is completed on time.
- Staying on target when those around you are distracting you from the end goal.
- Measuring success by how well the team/company does, not the individual.

The following pages contain a recent column from the "Words of Wisdom" newsletter from current CEO of Wisdom Adhesives, Jeff Wisdom. It typifies the can-do attitude of the company and its employees and is a great example of *The Wisdom Way*.

A WORD FROM THE CEO:
The Wisdom Way

The events of the last two years have brought tremendous challenges and opportunities to our organization that have never been seen in our 140 year history. Business is moving faster, volatility is higher and technology is changing ever-rapidly. Through these factors, Wisdom Adhesives remains grounded in its focus on serving our customers, attending to our valued employees and giving back to the communities in which we operate. We call this *The Wisdom Way*.

As an example, Wisdom Adhesives has traditionally served the bookbinding and graphic arts industries; however, change was necessary to keep up with the ever-moving landscape of these industries. The number of printed and bound books is projected to be relatively flat and stable for the next several years, but the advent of digital printing, on-demand publishing and e-books has transformed the industry in a way that will significantly influence the future of print media. We at Wisdom have changed with the demand of these companies by revamping our WizBind Bookbinding and our WizBond water-based adhesive lines to better match our customers' needs for faster turnaround, adhesion to non-traditional surfaces and ease of use on new binding equipment. In addition, we've also firmly established a global strategy to match the market needs.

Paraphrasing the words of John F. Kennedy, we ask not

what our customers can do for Wisdom, but what Wisdom can do for our customers. Adapting to a changing industry, like the bookbinding market, is key to our long-term viability. This is our core belief and it is one we adapt and strive to attain.

Thank you for your business.
Jeff Wisdom

Wisdom Green

Color has often been associated with prominent businesses or teams. IBM's "Big Blue" is one that comes immediately to mind. At Wisdom Adhesives, green has always been the "color" of choice, be it green from an environmental standpoint or green from the color of the branded Wisdom logo. "Proud to be Wisdom Green" dates back to the origins of the company and is the one color that represents *The Wisdom Way* and the six guiding principles, and it is depicted below in a recent marketing campaign.

To our customers—our lifeblood: Wisdom Green means Wisdom Adhesives Worldwide will sustain the highest standards of adhesives excellence in order to satisfy or exceed customer expectations daily, as we have since 1875.

To our employees—our lifeforce: Wisdom Adhesives Worldwide promises a lifetime of gainful employment, so long as our company sustains itself, in return for your hard work, high level of performance, and wisdom to keep Wisdom customers our number one priority.

To our communities—our lifework: Wisdom Adhesives Worldwide commits to supporting and giving back to the communities in which we operate, creating sustainable work environments and manufacturing environmentally-friendly and energy-efficient adhesive products.

Wisdom Green is The Wisdom Way to Succeed

Green is often associated with envy; however, there is little time for envy at Wisdom Adhesives, as the color green brings out Passion at Wisdom Adhesives.

PEARLS OF WISDOM:

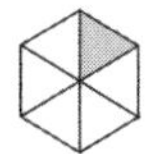 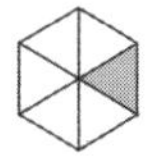 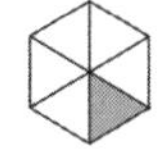 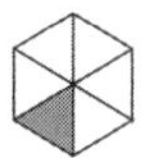 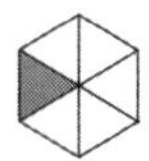 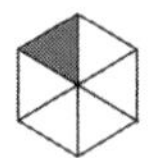

PASSION

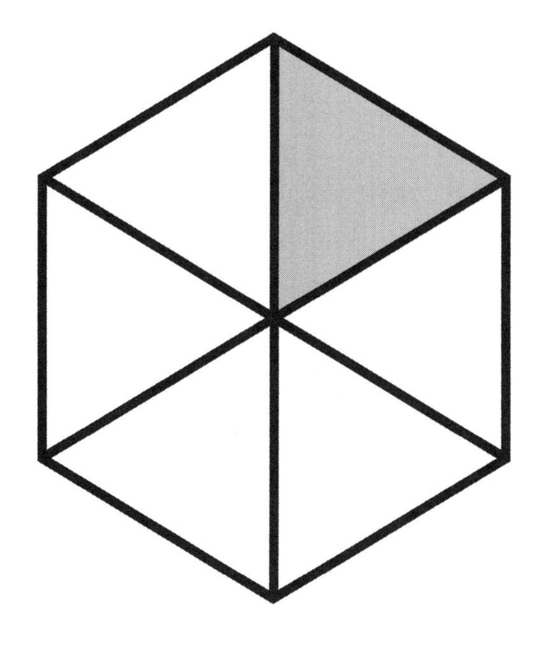

PASSION

Have Fire in Your Belly

"When you have passion and determination, you can accomplish anything."
Abraham Lincoln

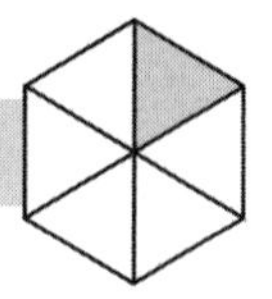

PASSION

In ancient Rome, when a person passed away, at the funeral gathering the value of that person's life was often judged by a single question:

Did they have passion?

If the Roman masses attending the funeral gave a thumbs up, indicating a yes, that person's life was considered a success. No reaction by those attending the funeral meant no Passion, thus a life that perhaps fell short.

Simply put, if people have Passion, they will likely be successful at their endeavors of choice. At Wisdom Adhesives, this is especially paramount. Passion can readily be seen in each and every business activity, employee, and response to customers. It is the intertwining of a multitude of efforts to persevere under good and, especially, bad times. Wisdom Adhesives started as a single entity back in 1875 and has grown into a global adhesive manufacturing company with reach to all corners of North America and the world. Passion is the fuel to supplying the engine of growth, sales figure growth that has exceeded over double digits for over the past decade.

In the mid-2000s, Wisdom introduced the concept of Efficient Compact Organization, with two levels of reporting from the shop floor to senior management. This business concept, known as the ECO^2 approach, gives responsibility and authority to the individual or team best prepared to make a quick decision.. ECO^2 allows for the organization to respond swiftly to all matters, especially those involving customers, employees, vendors, and the communities in which it operates. At the center of the ECO^2 concept is Passion. Passion is what drives an individual to, if needed, form a team to respond to a need.

In many ways,

$$ECO^2 = \text{Passion} = \text{Success}$$

It is something even Einstein would be proud of, as it is truly a mathematical equation. But it is a simple mathematical equation. As Passion increases, so does the desire to succeed. Success breeds further success, and soon you have an organization responding quickly to customer needs, in large part because of the Passion culture developed long ago.

Passion is fluid. People can be born with it and have it in their DNA, yet it is contagious and can spread to those less passionate. How many have seen this happen? Presumably, many. It takes great Passion at the leadership level to move an organization. Think of all the great countries, societies, military armies, businesses, and sports teams that have been successful mainly because of a passionate leader. At Wisdom Adhesives, Passion at the very top of the organization has been, and likely always will be, the driving force for the company.

If one has Passion, it is the first step in the direction of

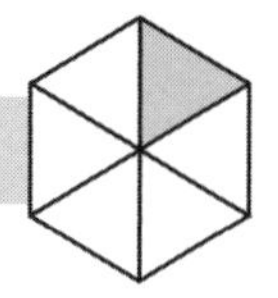

success in business or in life. Passion is the adhesive binding all the other concepts of *The Wisdom Way* together. Passion gives way to further Action. It spurs Reinvention. Passion provides Endurance. It gives strength to develop and cultivate Relationships and to continually provide Generosity.

Having Passion means:

- Be Passionate
- Have a Positive Outlook
- Know Your Business, Know Your Numbers
- Have Proper Etiquette
- Avoid Tap Dancing Around the Subject Matter
- Speak From the Heart
- Be Human
- Do What You Are Good at and Born to Do
- Know What You Are Not Good At
- Recognize Passion
- Have Self-Assurance
- Passion = Simplicity

If the question "Do they have Passion?" is asked of the leaders of Wisdom Adhesives or rank-and-file employees of Wisdom Adhesives, clearly, the ancient Romans would be putting their thumbs up.

Passionate: If You're Not, You Aren't Going Anywhere

THIS STATEMENT IS AS TRUE IN BUSINESS AS IN LIFE. THE more Passion you have the more you will get out of life. It can readily be put into a mathematical equation:

X amount of Passion = Y amount out of life

Increasing X will automatically increase Y. In order to increase Y, X will have to be increased. The lesson here is to be passionate in all your key endeavors.

Have Passion.

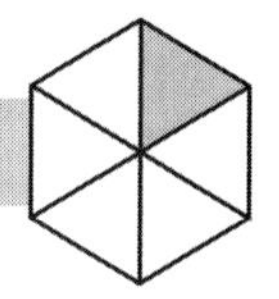

Be Positive, It's Contagious

BEING POSITIVE IS CONTAGIOUS. BEING POSITIVE within an organization promotes Passion. Being positive externally to customers promotes Passion. Many may not recognize it or even know it, but they gravitate to the positive if those around them are positive. A positive attitude begets a positive action.

Ask yourself this: How many positive people do you know who are passionate in their life and work? Nearly 100%. Then ask yourself this: How many of those people are successful? Again, the answer is likely 100%.

Be positive; be passionate.

Know Your Numbers and You Will Know Your Business

Know your numbers and you will know your business. You can speak with authority and provide confidence to others, and it's especially contagious.

The opposite is also true; if you don't know your numbers, you don't know your business.

Know your numbers passionately.

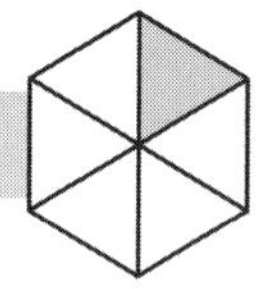

What's Your Etiquette?

WHAT'S YOUR ETIQUETTTE? THERE ARE MANY APPROACHES to life and to work. Determining the best path is an integral part of *The Wisdom Way*. One often thinks the best methods involve honesty, integrety, intent, and ultimatly, success when approaching a business opportunity. Maintaining a positive and passionate outlook shapes the etiquette for all to see.

A prime example would be to liken a golfer's use of proper etiquette to compete on a level playing field with competitors to that which can be used for business.

Your etiquette will determine your image and ultimately affect your business. Having good etiquette equates to good business. Good business is successful business. The same can be true of life. Have proper etiquette and you will have a good and successful life.

Let your etiquette determine your Passion.

Avoid the Tap Dance

Avoid the tap dance. When faced with a question, particularly from a valued customer, employee, or vendor, that you may not know the answer to, clear your thoughts and respond with a simple answer.

It is readily noticeable and many can see when you are making up the answer to simply fill space. If you don't know an answer, a simple "let me get back with you on it" is fair and realistic. Putting some Passion into your response can make the customer much more understanding and interested.

Avoid the dance; let Passion guide your response.

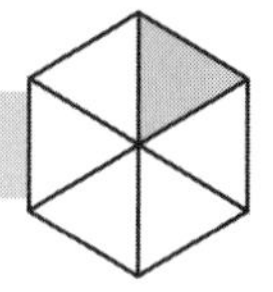

Speak From the Heart

Speak from the heart. Many meetings or business gatherings, especially conferences, are filled with formal presentations, typically in the form of PowerPoints. Speaking from the heart in an open forum could be your chance to be different, and you will be remembered. Speaking from the heart can show your Passion and knowledge of a subject.

There is a time for formality, but there is also a time for frankness. Speaking from the heart can emphasize your point. Adding a dash of Passion can imbed that point into the listener.

Speak from the heart with Passion.

Be Human

Be human. People respond to your vulnerability. "Sorry, I missed that" goes a lot farther than, "My secretary didn't give that to me."

Being human means being vulnerable. It means putting yourself out there for all to see. (Actually, it's like writing a book on *The Wisdom Way*.) Vulnerability makes for humanness, and generally, the responses have a positive effect.

Be human, have Passion.

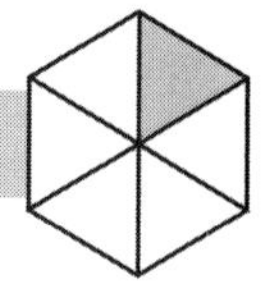

What You Are Good at Usually Isn't Too Far Off From What You Enjoy Doing

WHAT YOU'RE GOOD AT USUALLY ISN'T TOO FAR OFF FROM what you enjoy doing. This concept is attributed mainly to a high level of Passion. If you can sell well, you typically enjoy it. If you are an inventor and good at it, you enjoy it. Conversely, if you are bad at something, you generally don't enjoy it.

You can enjoy watching TV, but it's probably hard to make a living doing that. So find an occupation that you are good at, and generally, you will enjoy doing it.

What's next on your to-do list?

You can earn a pretty good living by having Passion.

Know What You're Good at and Recognize What You're Not Good At

KNOW WHAT YOU'RE GOOD AT AND RECOGNIZE WHAT you're not good at. Do more of the former and stay away from the latter. There's plenty of time in life to figure this out for yourself. The journey may just be its own reward.

If you can write, write. If you can sell, sell. If you can invent, invent. If you can service, service. If you can fix, fix. If you can't do, then don't. Life is simplified beyond belief.

If you have Passion, then be passionate.

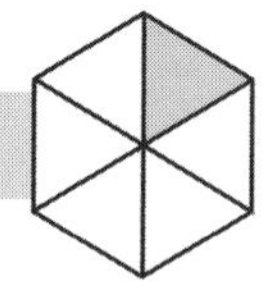

Passion Isn't Always Recognized, but It's Always Felt

Passion isn't always recognized, but it is always felt. Whether we know it or not, Passion is always around us; we just need to recognize it.

Have you ever had a great time at a restaurant, only to realize it was the high level of service you enjoyed? Conversely, restaurant disasters can readily happen when the service is poor and when Passion is nonexistent. Sometimes we may be too occupied to notice Passion, but when it is present, we are surely going to leave the experience richer than when we entered.

Passion is all around us; know where to look for it, as that is surely the place to be.

Be Happy with Self-Praise

BE HAPPY WITH SELF-PRAISE. MOST OF THE TIME, YOU have to be happy enough with self-praise and self-praise only. Most are too busy or too wrapped up in their own goings-on to recognize what a good job you may be doing. Learning to recognize this is an important step to *The Wisdom Way* becoming an integral part of your makeup.

Self-assurance will bolster your beliefs in what you are able to accomplish, making seemingly impossible tasks attainable. Self-assurance will give you the Passion needed to succeed, to reach the new sales goal, to develop the new product, to boldly go where no man has gone before. Self-assurance is the right amount of cockiness and not over confidence.

Self-praise is derived from self-assurance.

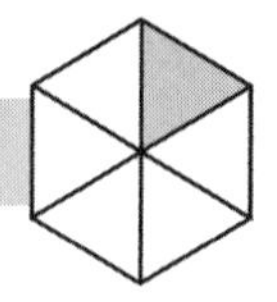

Passion = Simplicity

PASSION = SIMPLICITY. BREAKING DOWN YOUR BUSINESS or your life into simple segments and then developing a simple plan will result in a higher level of Passion. Having a high level of Passion will make your life and your business simpler.

There is much Passion in simplicity and there is much simplicity in Passion.

Simply have Passion, it's *The Wisdom Way*.

PEARLS OF WISDOM

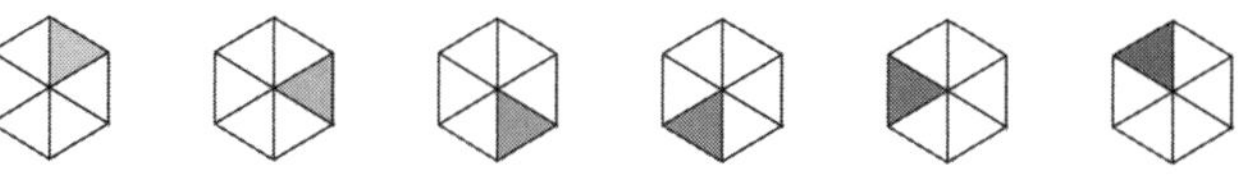
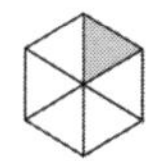
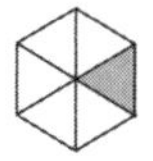
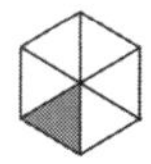
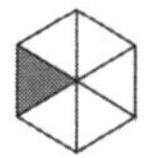
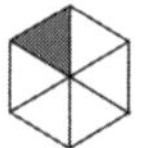

ACTION

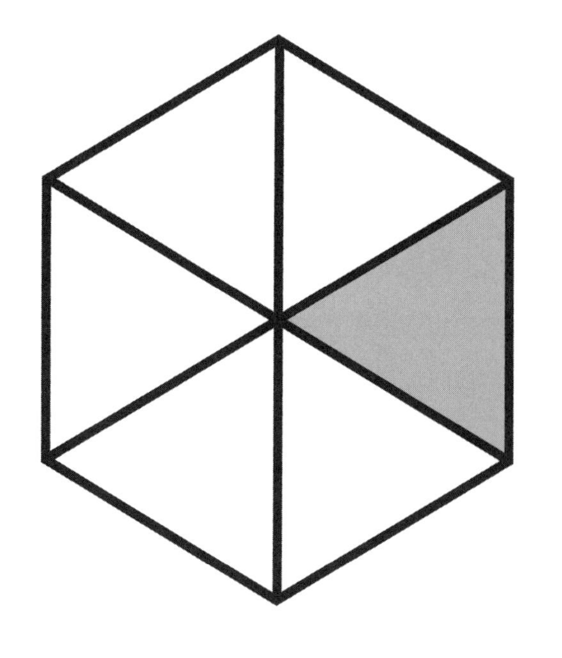

ACTION

Get It Done

"You are what you
do, not what you
say you'll do."
C. G. Jung

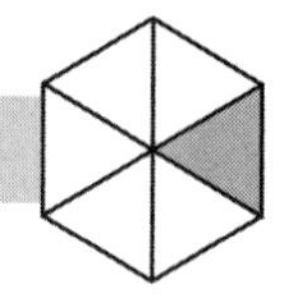

ACTION

THE OLD SAYING "ACTIONS SPEAK LOUDER THAN words" is so true today, in business and in life.

Action is the underlying strength of the success of Wisdom Adhesives. There are many instances were Action, quick Action, has stunted problems and created countless opportunities. At Wisdom Adhesives, Action is the name of game and has been since 1875, with:

- Solving customer problems, from shipping questions to product inquiries to quality questions to technical challenges

- Seizing opportunities, from being quick to participate in material opportunities to being the first to the customer on new or existing opportunities

- Expanding capabilities, from manufacturing to personnel moves

The realization of an ever-closing window on opportunities is the driving force for Action. The mentality of never resting on your laurels is as plainly seen today at Wisdom Adhesives as it has been for five generations.

Some examples of the Action mentality are:

- Keep customers supplied with material when no one else readily can, and do it in a timely manner.
- Develop a new or modified product at the desire or need of a customer.
- Custom formulate for customers and applications.
- Provide materials in specifically requested containers.
- Help customers through inventory requirements, using vendor-managed capabilities wherever needed.
- Economize on consumption of material through product development and/or on-site technical servicing.

Action is the fundamental principal of all for the success of Wisdom Adhesives. You don't get to be a five-generation company, nor survive for 140 years without Action. Key points of Action that have led to the formation of this principle of *The Wisdom Way* are:

- Sense of Urgency
- Act Like You Are Already There
- Be a Ship Business
- Block & Tackle
- Set the Market
- Overcome Friction
- Close While Fresh

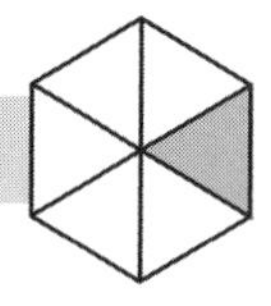

- Get an Early Win
- Move the Ball Forward
- Jump on a Plane
- Act Externally
- Performers Perform
- Act Like Your Customer
- Work Backwards
- Rapid Response
- But Don't Always Jump a Cliff
- Engage
- Let the Hole Develop

Doing something, moving the ball forward, and having the skill set to let the hole develop are all key components for taking the best Action in the most fundamental of key principles of *The Wisdom Way*.

Sense of Urgency

Hop in the car. Have a sense of urgency. Seize the day. Don't let time or momentum pass you by. If something needs doing, then do it. Don't put off for a minute that which could be done right now. It's advancing the ball at all times.

Have a sense of urgency; take Action.

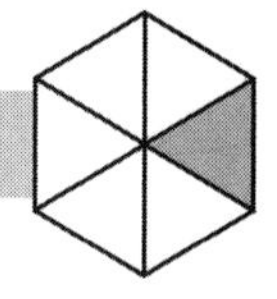

Act Like You're Already There

Act like you're already there. Business concepts and strategies should be in the spirit of where you want your company to be, not maybe where you are. An old tale tells of a Japanese company back in the 1980s that had a board meeting to discuss what their company would look like 100 years from that time. If you have an idea, carry yourself in such a manner that you are making decisions based on your new capabilities. In doing so, you are not only moving the timeline forward, but you are also creating a "dry run," essentially, testing the concept.

Act like you are already there and take Action.

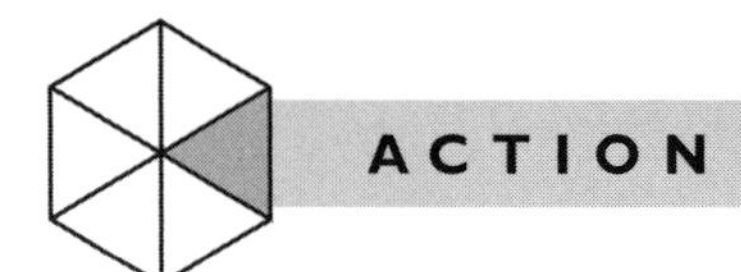

Be a Ship Business

BE A SHIP BUSINESS. BE AN ACTIVE PARTICIPANT IN THE market. Energize and solve the equation. Make doing business easier. Make business happen. Be a provider of solutions, opportunities, partnerships, and connections. In short, be a ship business.

Take Action and ship.

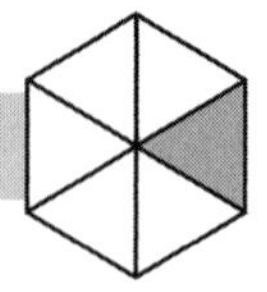

Block & Tackle

BLOCK AND TACKLE. DO THE FUNDAMENTAL TASKS IN business well and you will build a championship organization. The best football teams, like those of the Green Bay Packers in the 1960s, the Pittsburgh Steelers in the 1970s, and the San Francisco 49ers in the 1980s, all thrived and won championships by extreme attention to detail, executing the given plays—blocking and tackling. The exact same principles hold true for business: If you execute the basics well, the company will be a success and thrive in all environments. Conversely, if you do not execute the basics well, the company will be extinct in short order.

Basic tasks, such as taking an order, processing an order, manufacturing a product, or delivering a product, are all about blocking and tackling. They are about taking Action on the most basic types of tasks; however, doing them well will set the tone for the company to be successful and set the stage for the company to continue to grow.

Block and tackle. Take Action; it's *The Wisdom Way*.

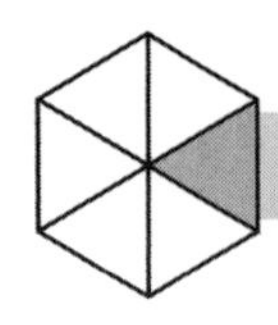

Set the Market

Setting the market is a specific idea used to quickly determine opportunities for success. Setting the market means selling a product or a service at the predetermined market price, regardless of your readiness to do so. You will know quickly if your idea or product is going to be well-received.

A customer once required substantial savings in order to change products and services. This savings was offered immediately, up front, while keeping the cost of the alternative product/service exactly the same. This actually caught the customer off guard, and they were at first hesitant to move forward, but ultimately proceeded. In essence, the customer wasn't initially ready to buy at the time, but provided the opportunity for the market to be set. Setting the market in this particular case allowed for reprioritizing, while saving time and money on the way to a successful venture.

In many cases, setting the market works to perfection. Opportunities give very clear guidance, which oftentimes can be readily met by setting the market.

Set the market. Take Action.

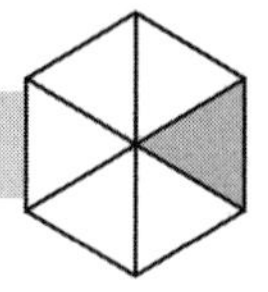

Friction Is a Reality

FRICTION IS A REALITY. THERE WILL ALWAYS BE FRICtion with Action. Think of friction as the red tape that prevents success. It must be overcome. There are two types of friction:

1. **Kinetic Friction.** This is the friction that continually tries to stop you from being successful on a project or a sale or, really, any endeavor. You're on your way to success, but there are constant roadblocks, or kinetic friction, that try to stop your advancement. The best way to defeat kinetic friction is to always be taking Action. Action is the demise of kinetic friction.

2. **Static Friction.** This is the friction that prevents you from even starting. Procrastinators are immersed in static friction. They never even get off the starting block. A higher level of Action is needed to overcome static friction, but once the hurdle is overcome, success will follow.

The best friction fighter is to take Action.

Get Closure While It Is Fresh

GET CLOSURE. DO IT WHILE IT'S FRESH IN YOUR MIND. If something is positive, get it done so you feel good. If something is negative, get it done to get rid of the negative energy. Either way, it requires Action.

The Wisdom Way is all about continually closing one chapter and starting another.

Get closure with Action.

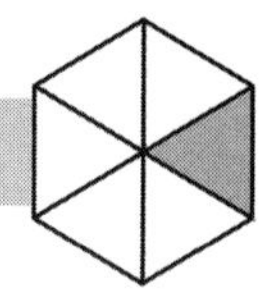

Get an Early W

W stands for Win. An early W will set the day. Start your morning with your list of things to do and do a task that you know you can accomplish. Don't start with the most difficult task, as it may kill your momentum for the day. Remember, wars are won one battle at a time. Knock out an attainable task right away and let the momentum build.

Get an early W. It sets the tone for your day. Take Action.

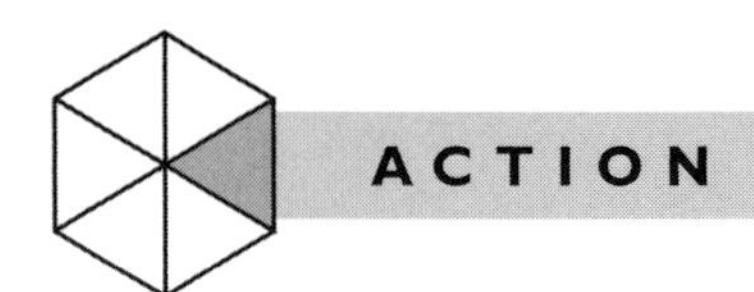

Move the Ball Forward

Move the ball forward. It is imperative to always be advancing business. Sales cycles, projects, and the like will take time to develop. One must constantly be developing methods for improving the quality of the product and presentation.

Moving the ball forward is critical to success and a very purposeful Action of *The Wisdom Way*.

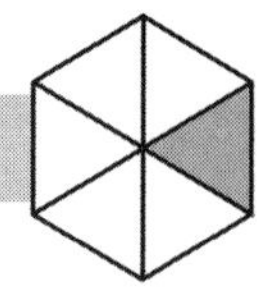

If All Else Fails, Get a Plane Ticket

IF ALL ELSE FAILS, GET A PLANE TICKET. IN THIS MODERN world of 24/7 communication, what can often be overlooked is the face-to-face meeting.

Back several years ago, there was this United Airlines commercial in which a business team was sitting around the table discussing how they had lost touch with their customers and how their sales showed clear evidence of decline. Clearly, something had to be done. At that point, the leader of the team pulled out a handful of airline tickets and proceeded to pass them out to each individual, indicating that each go see a customer face-to-face.

Taking Action, getting on a plane, it is *The Wisdom Way.*

What Happens in Vegas Doesn't Matter

What happens in Vegas doesn't matter. What happens internally doesn't matter. The only thing that really matters is how you present your company to your customers and that you are able to meet their needs.

All too often, organizations become too internally focused and lose track of why they organized in very first place.

What happens internally only matters if it prevents business from happening; otherwise, consider it table stakes.

Take Action externally.

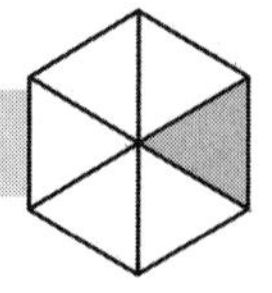

Performers Perform, Spectators Watch

PERFORMERS PERFORM, SPECTATORS WATCH. THERE IS no substitute for action; be a doer, not a watcher. It isn't necessarily that all there is to do is Action; it simply means, have a purpose to your plan. Taking Action is the key.

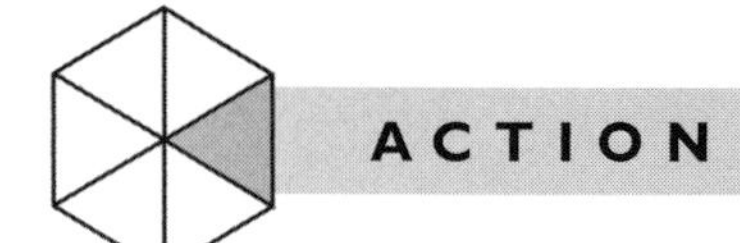

Act More Like Your Customers Than Your Vendors

ACT MORE LIKE YOUR CUSTOMERS THAN YOUR VENDORS. This has never been more true than in today's business world. Patterning your business in response to your customers often means acting like them. Patterning yourself after your vendors can often mean getting new vendors. Companies are in business to succeed and success comes from gaining customers. It's that simple, that straight forward.

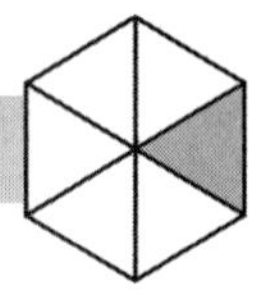

Work Backwards

WORK BACKWARDS. IF YOUR BUSINESS WANTS TO EARN $100,000 for a given time period, and you are only making $50,000 now, then set the goal and fill in the gaps. You don't need some elaborate scheme; just develop a framework and make it happen.

This same point, of course, can be applied to one's personal finances.

Take Action, work backwards.

Rapid Response, Even at Half-Strength, Is Better Than Waiting to Respond

Rapid response, even at half strength, is better than waiting to respond. It is better to respond immediately than to wait. You only have to be 50% correct responding right away, rather than being 100% correct but taking too long to respond. This is especially true for problematic situations. Customers want and deserve to know you will respond quickly. Often responding alone will suffice. Providing some information or solving some of the problem in an immediate fashion oftentimes is far better than methodically proceeding to solve the problem in its entirety. It simply may not be necessary to do so.

Respond rapidly, take Action.

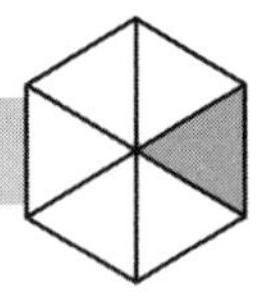

But Don't Always Jump

But don't always jump. Figure it out and then jump. Just because you respond immediately doesn't mean you should wing it. Respond immediately only when you have enough of your facts straight. A constituent wants to hear an answer from you when you have figured it out.

Prepare to take Action.

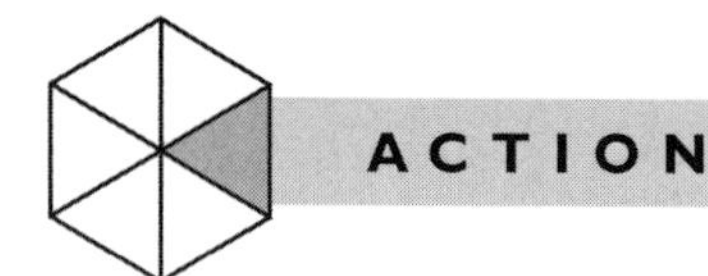

Engage

Engage. Be engaged in your business and in your life and you will be a success. Look from a distance for an extended period of time and you run the risk of failure. Heighten your engagement:

- During difficult times
- At the advent of a new undertaking, such as a project or new key hire
- With top accounts and prospects
- With the implementation of new key policies and procedures

Be engaged. Take Action *The Wisdom Way*.

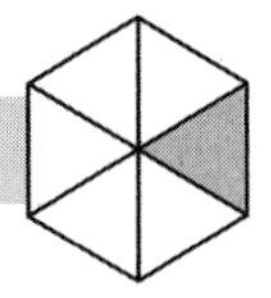

Let the Hole Develop

LET THE HOLE DEVELOP. OFTENTIMES, PICKING YOUR spots is the best method for accomplishment. Much like a great football running back, who must allow his blockers to do their jobs, one can provide the best Action when letting the hole develop.

Staying close to the situation is paramount. This will allow you to watch the goings-on and prepare yourself to act when the hole is developed. This takes a keen knowledge of the subject and a willingness and "gut-feel" to go ahead.

Letting the hole develop and then taking decisive Action when the right, opportune time is upon you is critical for success and a foundation of *The Wisdom Way*.

PEARLS OF WISDOM:

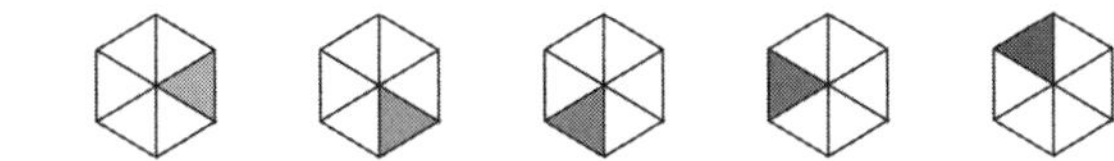
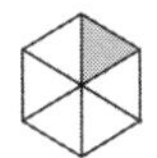
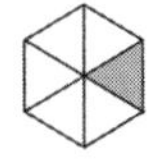
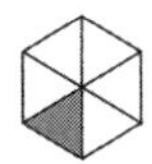
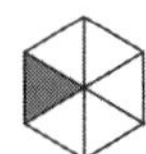
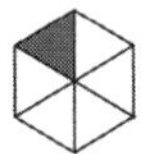

REINVENTION

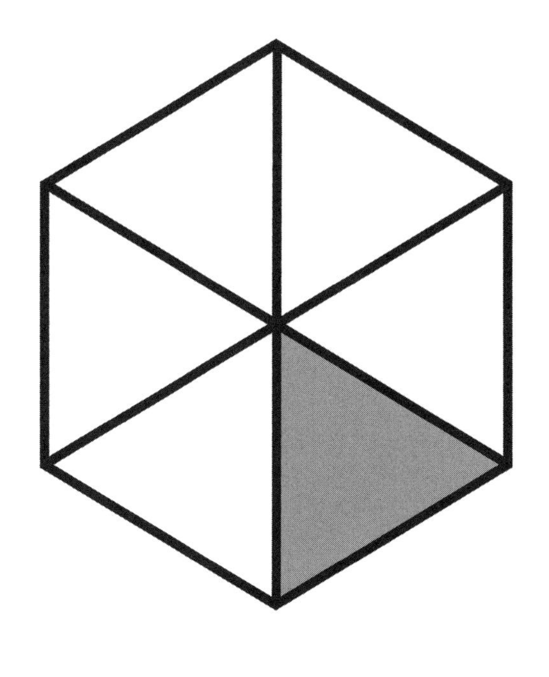

REINVENTION

Think Outside the Box

"Don't be afraid to go out on a limb. That's where the fruit is."
H. Jackson Browne

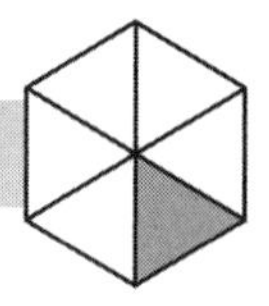

REINVENTION

Anyone can do well in good times; it is during the rough times that one shows his or her true colors. It was important than during the recession of 2007–2009 for Wisdom Adhesives to show its true colors. Their performance during this period was a continuation of double-digit growth, bolstered mainly through laser-like concentration on the core business, matching manufacturing, service, and sales to these precise goals.

During this rough business climate, Wisdom continued to pursue the fundamental principles of *The Wisdom Way*. Next is a message from the CEO of Wisdom Adhesives showing the guiding light to reinvent during this time of, not despair, but opportunity.

A WORD FROM THE CEO:

Winter/Spring 2008/2009 CEO Column

Down to Business ...

I AM REMINDED OF A TIME NOT LONG AFTER I STARTED WORKING in the adhesives industry when all the news and talk of the day was about how economically bad things were in our country. Many of my college classmates had a very hard time finding work; some stayed on and went to graduate school, as there were simply not enough positions for the amount of new graduates coming into the workforce. Sound familiar? It was a couple of decades ago, but our country and countries around the world are going through the same seemingly cyclical economic environment. I remember thinking back then as I do today, much is out of my control; the only thing I can do was get down to business. Getting down to business is *The Wisdom Way*.

Back then I was essentially a greenhorn in the adhesives world. Today, as I look back, Wisdom Adhesives has become the top mid-sized adhesive company, and the meaning of green for me has changed, becoming a Wisdom flagship product line name—GreenBond Sustainable Adhesives. The lesson I take from this is as follows–set aside ideas and relations that will not adapt to the ever-changing times. Reinvention is the key. Now more than ever, companies are

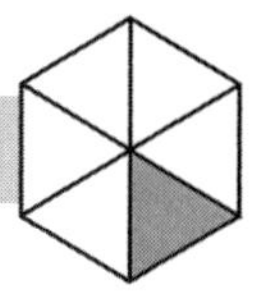

required to be nimble, ever-changing and current. We at Wisdom Adhesives have developed a Sustainable Charter in which we are constantly challenged and reminded of the need to change and the need to adapt to meet our customers' requirements. The Sustainable Charter forces us to adapt to the current situations. For instance, in the automotive industry, automobiles are produced, sent to dealers and typically sit on a lot trying to be sold.

In these economic times, this system seems antiquated. Why not have just a few cars of each model in the showroom for test driving, etc. ... then sit down with the prospective buyer and build the car to suit for delivery in two weeks. Our Sustainability Charter long ago allowed us to make custom products at competitive pricing to meet the needs of our customers.

Thank you for your business.
Best Regards,
Jeff Wisdom

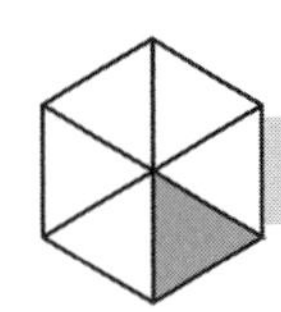

REINVENTION

Reinvention has always been the mother of invention at Wisdom Adhesives and an integral principle of *The Wisdom Way*. The keys to Reinvention are:

- Knowing the Trigger Point
- Being an Asset
- Avoiding Negativity
- Striving for Your Goal
- Understanding That the Winning Horse Uses the Least Energy
- Recognizing Accomplishments When You Arrive at a Destination

Those who sit on their laurels will pay a high price in business and in life. Reinventing to constantly changing conditions will allow one to thrive. It's *The Wisdom Way*.

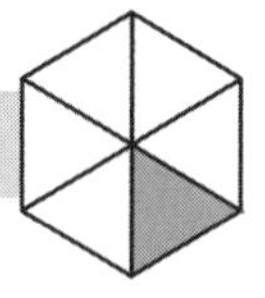

What Is the Trigger Point

WHAT IS THE TRIGGER POINT? TOO OFTEN WE SHOOT from the hip. Got an idea? Communicate it. Next, build on the idea. Develop some action items. Then further build the idea. When you reach the trigger point—and three or four or five reasons to support the idea—then Act. In doing so, your idea has more meat on the bone, and you can much more easily navigate or sell it.

Reinvention is to Action what new customers are to sales. One must reinvent by finding the trigger point for when to do so.

Cold Calls Are for Saps

Cold calls are for saps; being an asset is the key. If a customer wants to buy from you, they are likely going to find you and know who you are. How well do you position yourself, your product, and/or your company so customers come to you? That is the key. You can do this by knowing your subject and knowing it well so customers will come to you. Being a resource, problem solver, and asset is most critical. Offering a price is often not.

Cold call if you must, but perhaps consider reinventing to be an asset.

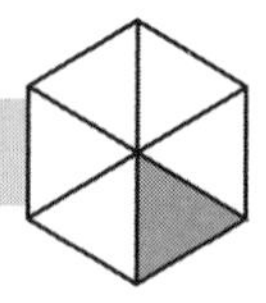

Avoid Negativity

Avoid the negative. Let's say you can't do something. "Give me one ton of widgets that are blue." Answer in a way that sells versus scrambles. "French vanilla isn't blue, but it's our best seller."

Responding in a positive fashion, no matter the communication type, is always a winner. Present yourself as such.

Call into Wisdom Adhesives, and you will be answered by a live person greeting you with, "It's a great day at Wisdom." It's the way life should be. Tomorrow isn't promised to any of us, be it your business or your life.

Avoid the negative, it's *The Wisdom Way.*

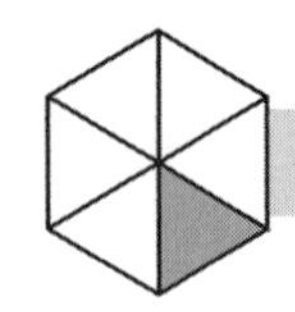

Strive for Your Goal

Strive for your goal, not theirs. Chicago is a city of 10 million people. One hundred thousand are super rich, 900,000 are poor and destitute. The other 9 million are desperately trying to be like the 100,000. You don't have to be one of them.

Be an independent, a contrarian, a not-go-with-the-crowd guy. Reinvent yourself; it's critical for life and business survival.

Strive for your goal, not someone else's. Reinvent.

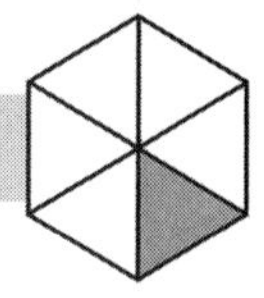

The Winning Horse Uses the Least Energy

The winning horse uses the least amount of energy. Think of it, the winning horse can win the race but not necessarily have to expend all its energy in doing so; however, a losing horse can expend every single solitary ounce of energy and still lose the race.

The winning horse wins with natural talent, hard work, and preparation, continually challenging itself, developing the best course of action to take, and then simply going out and winning the race.

Be a winning horse. Reinvent.

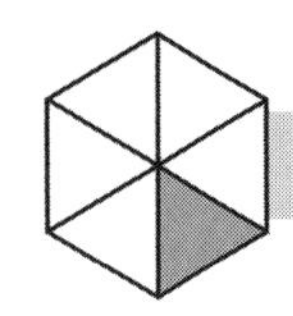

Look at the Accomplishment When You Get There

Look at the accomplishment when you get there. Instead of planning on top of planning, sometimes it's good to do one thing then see what it looks like when you get there. This might not work when playing a game of chess, but it can work when you're tackling a major project.

It is more important to look at the accomplishment once you get there, versus heavy planning and never allowing the Action and probable Reinvention to occur. Getting from point A to point B is rarely a straight line in life or business.

Know where you are going, but be confident that if you get off track, you can recognize the accomplishments along with way. Reinvent.

PEARLS OF WISDOM:

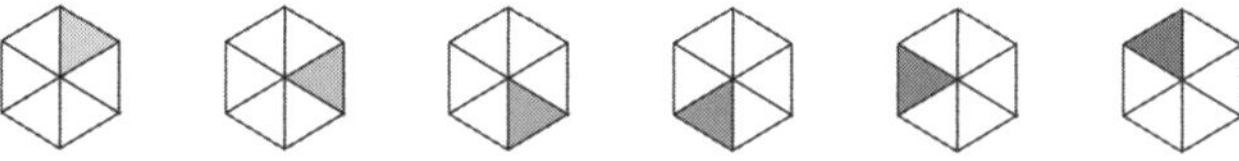
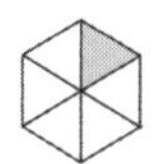
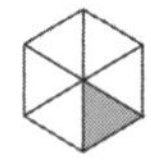
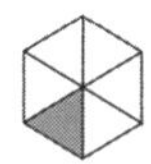
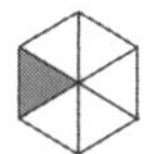
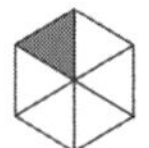

ENDURANCE

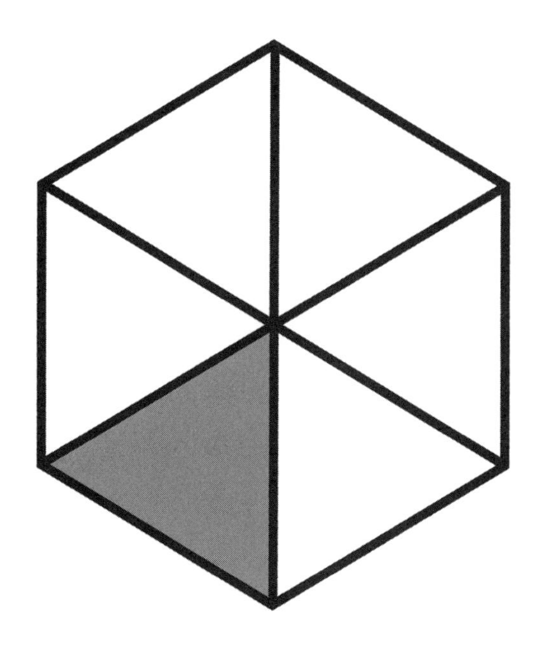

ENDURANCE

Stick to It

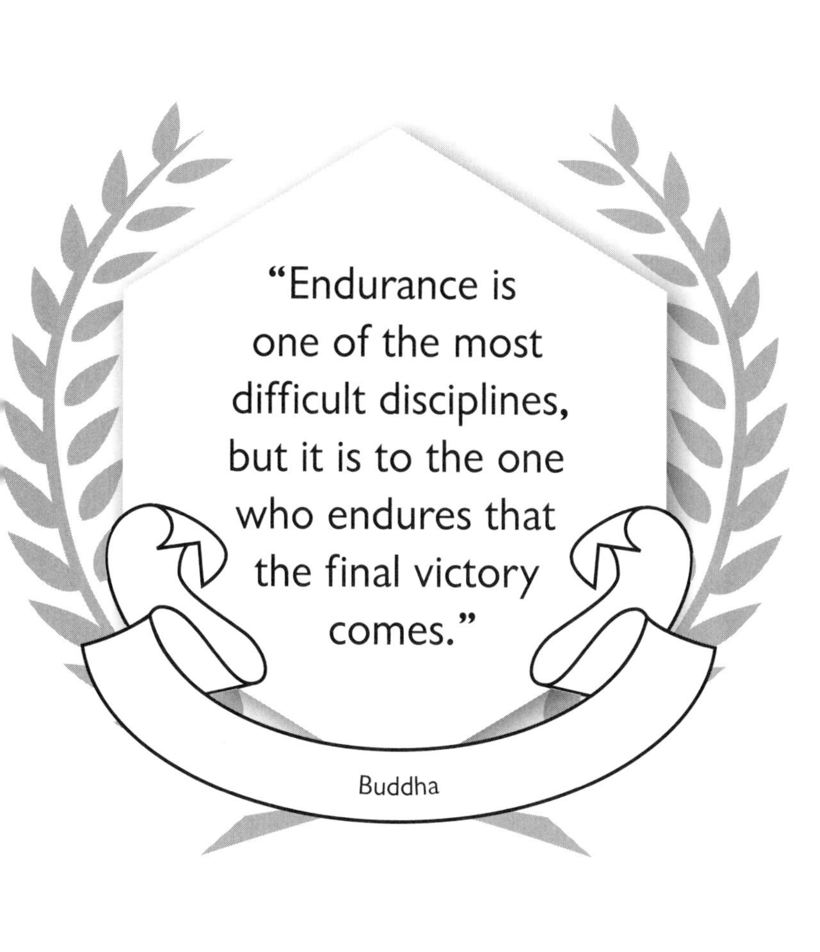
"Endurance is
one of the most
difficult disciplines,
but it is to the one
who endures that
the final victory
comes."
Buddha

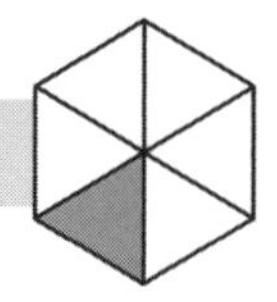

ENDURANCE

Go Pre. You may or may not have heard of one of the all-time greatest long-distance runners in the history of our country and the world. His name was Steve Prefontaine. Pre, as he was known to all who followed the sport, had a storied career as a middle- to long-distance runner, at one time holding all American records, from anything over half a mile to the marathon. Pre's approach was to go all out at all times in a race, and may the best man win. He had the heart of a champion, and it took a more talented runner with a heavy dose of guts to beat Pre. In a nutshell, Pre evenly represents *The Wisdom Way*. Passion, Action, and Endurance were key components to Pre's success and are cornerstones to *The Wisdom Way*. Pre's career was cut short by a late-night, single-car traffic accident on a dark and winding road. Ironically, he was in the process of Reinventing himself for the upcoming 1976 Olympic Games in Montreal. He never got the chance, but one can only imagine the brilliance he would have displayed.

Pre's actions were in a microcosm, like those of Wisdom Adhesives throughout the years.

What follows is another president's column, written

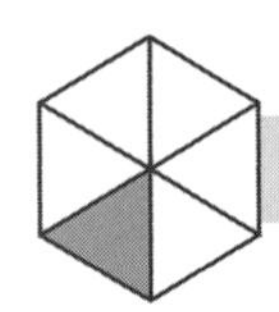

around the time of the recession in 2008 by the CEO/President of Wisdom Adhesives. It clearly demonstrates the continuing fortitude of Endurance necessary to sustain during those dark and rumbling times.

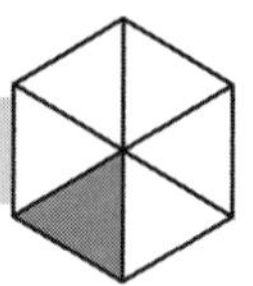

A WORD FROM THE CEO:

Dear Customers, Employees and Communities of Wisdom Adhesives:

As the new year begins, we at Wisdom Adhesives would like to restate our Mission Statement:

Our value unique proposition is at the core of our business: *The Wisdom Way—Putting the Customer First.*

We believe we have a very unique business proposition that says simply—"Sets Wisdom Apart from the Competition," and it is as follows:

Wisdom Adhesives Business Proposition is governed by the 3Bs—

- BEST IN TECHNOLOGY—For the products we manufacture and sell
- BEST IN INDUSTRY SERVICE & SALES—Optimum pricing, ability to contain costs, continuous improvement, adapting and keeping ahead of market trends
- BEST IN CLASS OPERATION—Supporting sales and R&D for 133 years

These three ideas above are bolstered by our everlasting endurance to go it for the long haul. Trust and know that Wisdom Adhesives will be there for you for the longest of hauls.

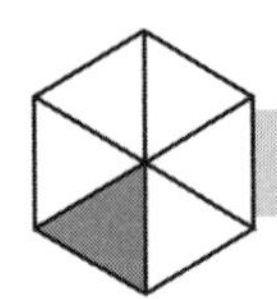

Please let us show you and continue to show how *The Wisdom Way* is truly the best in the adhesives industry.

Thank you for your business.
Best Regards,
Jeff Wisdom

ENDURANCE

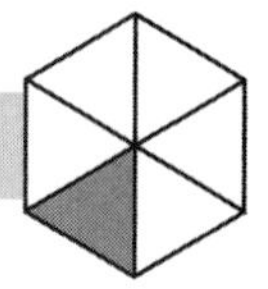

Having Endurance means using the following concepts:

- Less Is More
- Swim Like a Duck
- Be a Hitter
- Know When to Rest
- No Opportunity Is Ever Over
- Earn It

Having Endurance in one's life is as important as having knowhow. A smart person can be outdone by a less smart person solely based on the ability of the less smart person to have greater Endurance. It's the ideal equalizer in the business world, as depicted in the following equation.

Success = Smarts x Opportunity x Endurance

The more Endurance, the greater the success. It's *The Wisdom Way.*

Less Is More

Less is more. Work smarter not harder. Less is more is one of the most singularly important concepts of *The Wisdom Way*. By performing a task in the most efficient manner possible, by going from point A to point B with as little deviation as possible, one can maximize output while minimizing cost.

Less is More yields *Maximum Output* at the *Lowest Cost*.

This has been the mantra of *The Wisdom Way* since its foundation in 1875. Less is more has been applicable in robust times, when resources are in abundance, and lean times, when less is more is a necessity, both adding to the Endurance of the organization.

The less is more concept has been applied to:

- The development of product lines capable of increasing usage while minimizing consumption and costs.
- The use of key manufacturing resources in a multitude of ways, conserving both capital and foundation space.

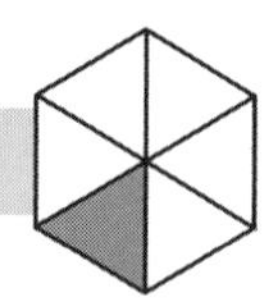

- The use of personnel in all facets of the organization, from R&D to manufacturing to procurement to sales and management, serving multiple disciplines to create an environment capable of successfully carrying on *The Wisdom Way* culture. A prime example of this is the ECO^2 approach, where decisions, accountability, and rewards are placed at the personnel level, where staff is capable of carrying out the task.

The less is more approach is such an effective concept that it has been in play with companies, governments, and individuals for many years. Those embracing the concept will find themselves flourishing. Those who do not embrace the less is more mentality often find themselves behind the productivity curve and lacking the Endurance to carry on.

Less is more. Endurance. *The Wisdom Way.*

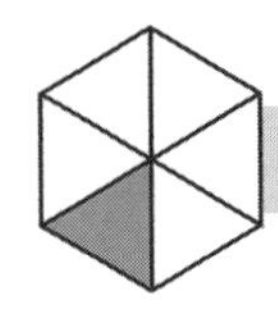

Swim Like a Duck

Swim like a duck. A duck swims easily on the surface, but paddles hard below the surface. Underneath is what you're company is doing to make sure the business floats, much like a duck. Having the right personnel in place under the right situation will allow the company to succeed. Be prepared and have the Endurance to swim.

Swim with Endurance.

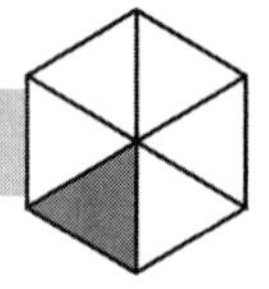

Be a Hitter

BASEBALL HITTERS ARE SUCCESSFUL BY HITTING JUST one out of every three. Think of it, one hit out of three at bats and you're on your way to the Hall of Fame. The best hitters average just over 0.300. The best sales guy is going to sell one for every three. Embrace these odds. Swing and miss twice, smile, and then enjoy and go after your hit.

Have the Endurance to take many swings.

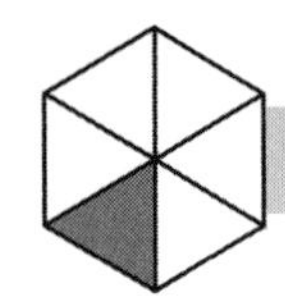

Know When to Rest

KNOW WHEN TO GIVE IT A REST. SOMETIMES NOT BEING able to finish a project is a blessing in disguise. If it isn't coming together, give it a rest, then come back to it. Having the skill to know when to rest and when to go hard will give you the Endurance you need over the long haul. Business and life are marathons, not sprints.

Knowing when to rest and when to go hard will provide fuel for the long haul and provide Endurance.

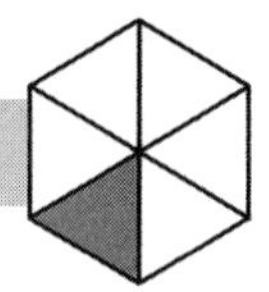

No Customer Is Ever Lost

No customer is ever lost. Turn a negative into a positive, even if it takes years to do so. Be in it for the long haul. What might not happen today, have the Endurance to go after tomorrow. Always, always, always leave the door open for a comeback. It will happen if you have the Endurance.

Keep active, be a resource, provide alternative products and methods. Have Endurance.

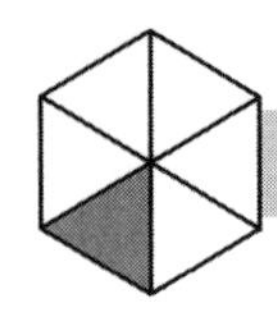

Earn It

Earn it. Work before play. A beer tastes better after you've worked for it, not first thing in the morning. Make this a habit and you will be a success in life and business.

Earn it, then play. Have Endurance.

PEARLS OF WISDOM:

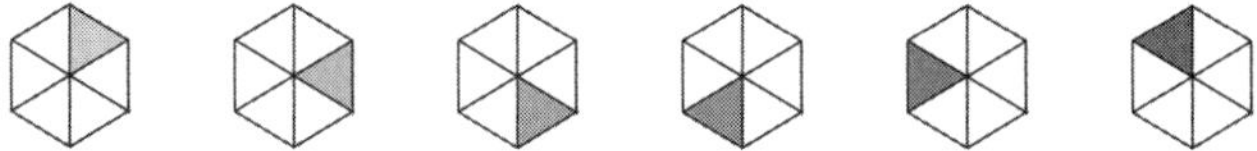
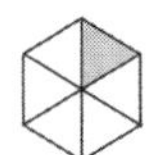
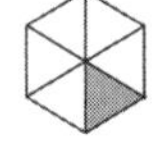
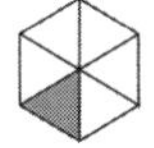
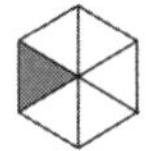
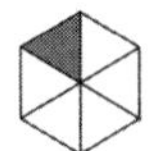

RELATIONSHIPS

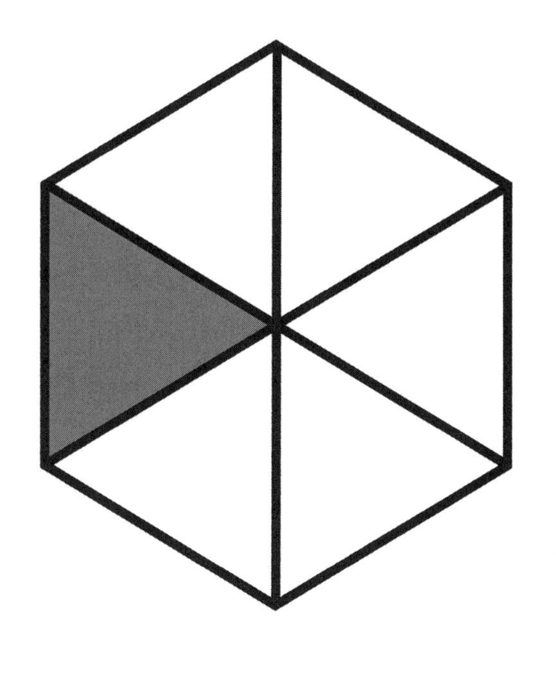

RELATIONSHIPS

Build Strong Connections

"The greatest
ability in Business
is to get along
with others."
John Hancock

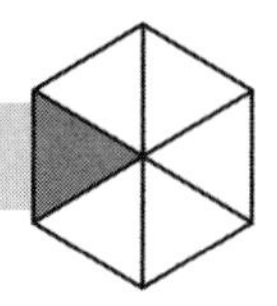

RELATIONSHIPS

No business can operate without relationships.

No person can live or function without relationships.

At some point in your life, career, or business, you will need the assistance of someone close to you to carry the ball in your time of need.

In your personal life, it may be a close friend, a spouse, or significant other helping you in your time of need. Let's face it, from a personal perspective, most problems are health related or finance related.

In your career, relationships often prove to be the intangible. If you're young, find a mentor. A mentor will guide you through the unnecessaries and get you to be proficient at the necessaries.

In business, customers, employees, and vendors are key. Customers are the backbone of the business. It is essential to have great relationships with your customers. Managing employees can be the toughest and most thankless task in a business. It's necessary to have good working relationships with subordinates, colleagues, and superiors. These relationships will differ but are all necessary for success. Vendors are necessary to keep your business supplied and serviced. A good vendor will pull you out of jams that you otherwise could not get out of.

Building and maintaining good Relationships is key and can be helped by:

- Making Yourself Available
- Knowing Who You Are Dealing With
- Rewarding the User
- Being a Psychologist
- Macronizing It
- Firing a Customer?
- Location, Location, Location
- Mixing the Technology Cocktail
- Picking Up the Phone
- Sales Funnel and the Glacier
- Disarming the Issue, Making It Right
- *The Wisdom Way*
- Bananas Grow on Trees, Customers Don't
- 50% of Selling Is One-Half Mental
- Respect, Mon
- Being Like Butch and Sundance

Relationships are key to your business. Relationships are key to your life. Developing the right ones at the right time are integral for success.

Build key Relationships, it's *The Wisdom Way*.

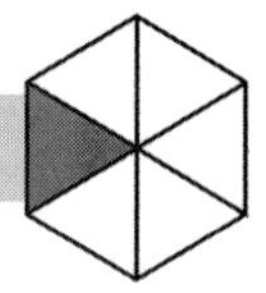

Anytime After a Little While

ANYTIME AFTER A LITTLE WHILE. MAKE YOURSELF AVAILable anytime, anywhere. Give yourself time to prepare, build, and enhance the relationship. Being accommodative to the relationships that will help you profit is critical for success.

Anytime After a Little While. Build the relationships that will help you most. It's integral for success and a part of *The Wisdom Way*.

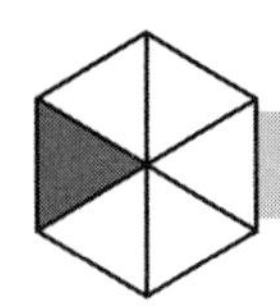

Know Who You're Dealing With

Know who you're dealing with. If you expect the world but are dealing with a non-world provider, you will not succeed. It's important to know who you are dealing with. This can be readily accomplished with knowing where you are going and who can best help you to get there.

Bringing in an expert when it is critical is paramount to success. Knowing who the experts are and having Relationships with them can provide you with unprecedented success.

Success = Limited Number of High Quality Relationships x Expertise of Relationships

Know who you are dealing with, have the Relationships.

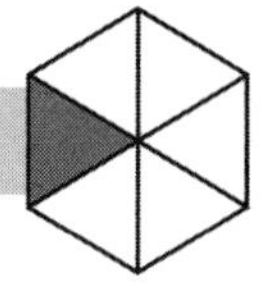

Reward the User

Once you have the business, reward people using the product, not the ones buying the product. There was a manufacturer in the Northeastern United States in the 1950s who'd put a Morgan silver dollar in every can of glue. As the users on the line would get down to the bottom of the can, the dollar would start rattling around and offer a nice little gift, a thank you for using it. He never lost any business using this method.

Don't just win over the purchasing department or supervisor, but win over the team.

Reward the user, have the Relationship.

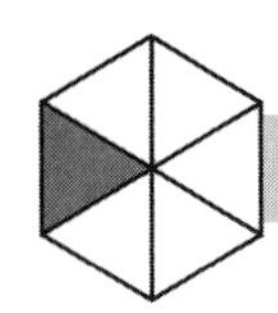

Psychologist vs. Salesman

Psychologist versus salesman. Psychologists have it easy. Psychologists can tell a patient what's wrong with them and often be lauded and thanked for doing so. Salesmen have it tough. A customer has a bad weekend, has employee issues, whatever, they can easily take it out on you. If you call them on it, you are likely to create an unwanted issue. Worse, you can lose the business. It's better to get on their level and understand when to go forward with discussions and when not to. Play the role that is needed at the time.

Be a psychologist or whatever you need to be or can be with constituents. Have the Relationship to do so.

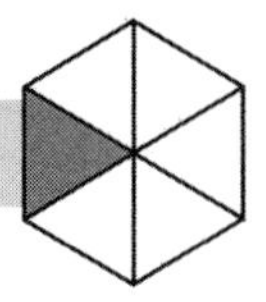

Macronize It

Give an analogy. Macronize it. A macro example can be understood more readily. Then drill down to the specific opportunity or issue. Present in a way all can understand. Build the bigger picture. Smaller issues can tend to be eliminated.

Macronize where possible; develop key Relationships that allow you to do so.

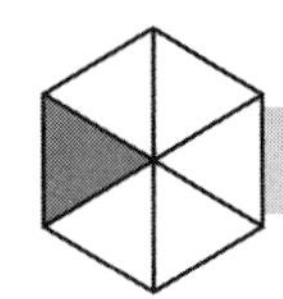

Fire a Customer?

Fire a customer? As a seller, you can set the limit. Once in a great while, you will have a customer that won't let you succeed. In those instances, you may be unable to make a profit or unable to gain any strategic value, yet you spend valuable resources. Know when to cut your losses, but keep the door open; as times change, people change.

Fire a Customer? Have the Relationship to do so.

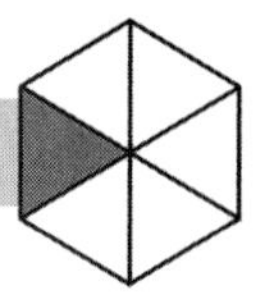

Location, Location, Location

WHAT ARE THE THREE MAIN THINGS IN REAL ESTATE? Location, location, location. In business, it's local, local, local. Everybody wants to feel like they are the only customer. You have to give them that local service.

Be local, have the Relationship.

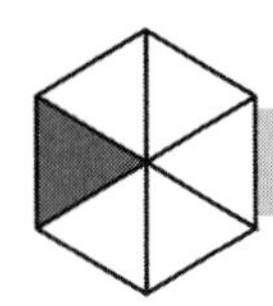

Mix the Cocktail

Mix the cocktail. With all of today's technology, it's easy to over serve one. Email everybody, only use the phone, or only see them in person. Determine which mix works best for a given Relationship, and do more of that.

Customize the communication cocktail. Some customers respond best by email. Others don't know how to open their email and only respond to phone calls. How often should you go see a customer? Is texting a customer out of line? There are no absolutes or right answers. The best way to communicate with a customer is to treat everyone differently and mix the cocktail to what works with each. The endgame isn't for them to like you or think you're Superman. The endgame is results. With so much to do in a day, it's a waste of time to mix the wrong communication cocktail and hope they respond to it. Don't know how to best communicate with a customer? Ask them. Don't know how often a customer wants to be seen face-to-face? Ask them.

Mix the cocktail, have the Relationship.

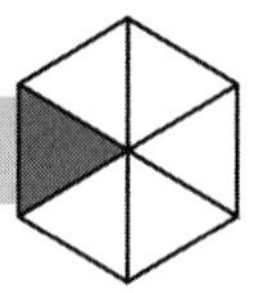

Pick Up the Phone

PICK UP THE PHONE, MAKE THE CALL, AND BUILD THE Relationship. In today's world, hiding behind technology can be bad for business. Knowing the best avenue to pursue for the communication cocktail is paramount for a successful Relationship.

Pick up the phone. It's *The Wisdom Way*.

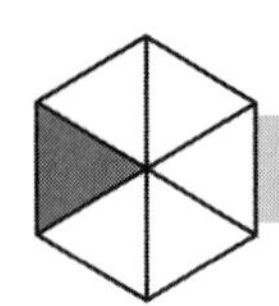

Sales Funnels and the Glacier Effect

Sales funnels and the glacier effect. Glaciers are unique in that the exposure above water is a minor part of the greater whole. In business, treat every customer like they are on the exposed-above-waterline part of the glacier. They don't need to see, know, or feel your business below the waterline.

The only Relationship the customer wants is with you, so make that Relationship a priority.

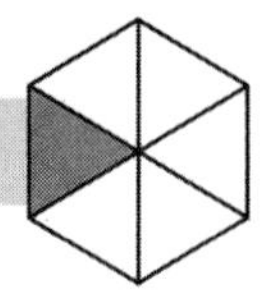

Disarm the Issue, Make It Right

When going into an issue, disarm the situation by initially saying you are going to make it right, and then proceed to lay out how you are going to do so. Issues will happen; be prepared. All you have to really rely on is your Relationship with those involved. It is an excellent time to build that Relationship. Most will appreciate what you have done when you do what you say you are going to do in resolving an issue. The bond will be stronger.

The strength of a relationship is proportional to the success in a quick resolution.

Use the ECO^2 approach: Disarm the issue, make it right and build the Relationship. It's *The Wisdom Way*.

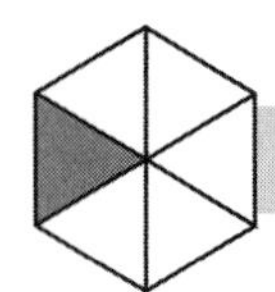

The Wisdom Way

The Wisdom Way is all about 1) customers, 2) employees, and 3) the communities in which the organization operates and does business. Relationships with all three constituents are the key to success in business.

The Wisdom Way is all about Relationships. It's key to doing business and key to life in general.

Embrace these Relationships, it's *The Wisdom Way*.

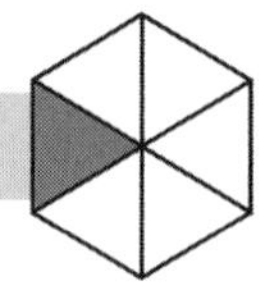

Bananas Grow on Trees, Customers Don't

Bananas grow on trees, customers don't. Cherish each and every customer. It is the reason why you are in business. Please, don't ever, ever forget this.

Have the Relationship. It's *The Wisdom Way*.

50% of Selling Is One-Half Mental

Fifty percent of selling is one-half mental. Actually, 50% of selling is 90% Relationship. Knowing the customer, being local, and developing the Relationship are key to success.

Everyone liked the New York Yankee catcher Yogi Berra and he won the most World Series of anyone. Emulate it.

Have the Relationship.

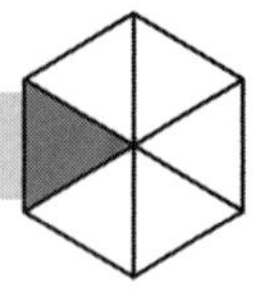

Respect, Mon

Respect, mon. You don't have to be a Rastafarian on the beach in Jamaica to understand "respect, mon." The opposite of this includes long-winded voicemails, self-indulgent emails, or talking about yourself until you're out of breath. Nobody cares. What people care about is the golden rule.

Treat others as you would like to be treated.

No matter what, everyone deserves respect.

Have respect, develop the Relationship.

EFFECTIVE TEAMS ...
Be Like Butch and Sundance

Be like Butch and Sundance. Many have seen the movie *Butch Cassidy and the Sundance Kid.* It is the story of two bank robbers who formed the ultimate partnership and, in many ways, embraced the six key principles of *The Wisdom Way.* Butch and Sundance's ability to work together embodies the Relationship principle of *The Wisdom Way* in its truest form.

The partnership formed by Butch and Sundance typifies the principles of business where Passion, Action, Reinvention, Endurance, Relationships, and Generosity are all key components of any successful venture. As you can readily see from the following summary, they actually were practicing the six principles of *The Wisdom Way.*

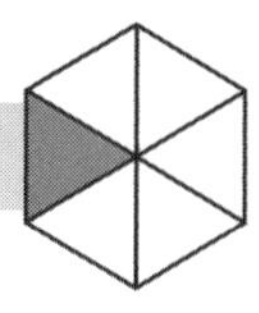

Used with permission from Inmagine.

Butch and Sundance's Ultimate Team:

Passion—It was obvious from the start of the movie that Butch and Sundance had a passion for bank robbing. They did what they loved to do, mainly because they were good at it. Butch was the brains; Sundance was the skilled gunslinger. Together they were unbeatable.

Action—Clearly Butch and Sundance were about Action. When money ran low, they opted to rob another bank. When times were good, they rested and honed their skills. When they needed to learn a different language, they studied. When they were being chased by bounty hunters, they always kept one step ahead by constantly being on the move and taking Action. Keeping up with the times was key to the success and survival.

Reinvention—Changing, or Reinventing, served the duo well. When they needed to make a move from the United States to a faraway place, they moved to Bolivia to rest and recuperate and eventually get back to the business of robbing banks. It's what they did and who they were. Their partnership was put to the test many times, but they always relied on each other. Just prior to moving to Bolivia, there was the

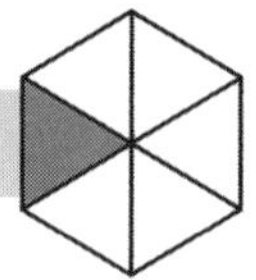

scene where they were cornered on a mountain top and the only escape was to jump from a high cliff into a raging stream. They did it, even though Sundance could not swim. He Reinvented and became a make-shift swimmer and trusted Butch would assist, as he did.

They were masters at improvising and Reinvention.

Endurance—Butch and Sundance, without a doubt, had Endurance. They evaded the law for all of their careers, often by outlasting the opponent. This was key for Butch and Sundance but is also key to any business endeavor. Be prepared for the long haul. Butch and Sundance were.

Key to their Endurance was choosing to do what they were good and skilled at. They knew their strengths and limitations, and by working together, they were able to accomplish much more than if they worked alone or strayed from their plans.

Relationships—Butch and Sundance were partners to the end. Their admiration for each other is a lesson for all for building a working Relationship. They had fun when they could and worked hard when they needed to. Butch and Sundance's Relationship is intertwined in the six Key Principles of *The Wisdom Way* and they were masters at it.

Generosity—In many ways, the duo was like Robin Hood: They oftentimes they took on the underdog role and were admired by many of those they took "business" from. Their Generosity helped build their future success.

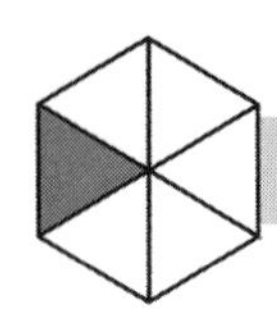

See the movie again. You will agree there are classic lessons to be learned, many of which align with *The Wisdom Way* principles.

Relationships are important to your business. Choose them wisely.

PEARLS OF WISDOM:

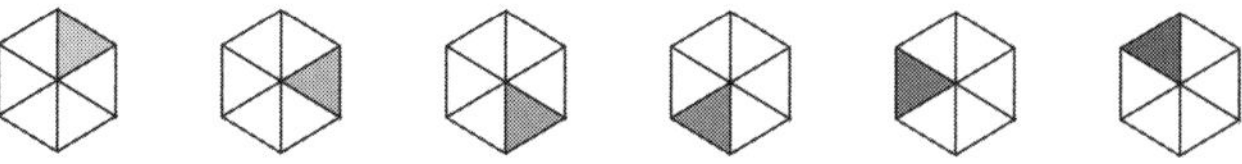
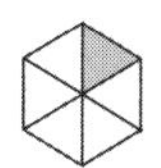
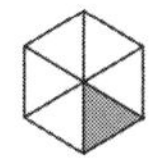
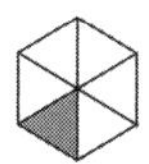
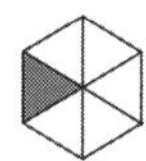
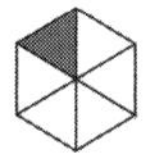

GENEROSITY

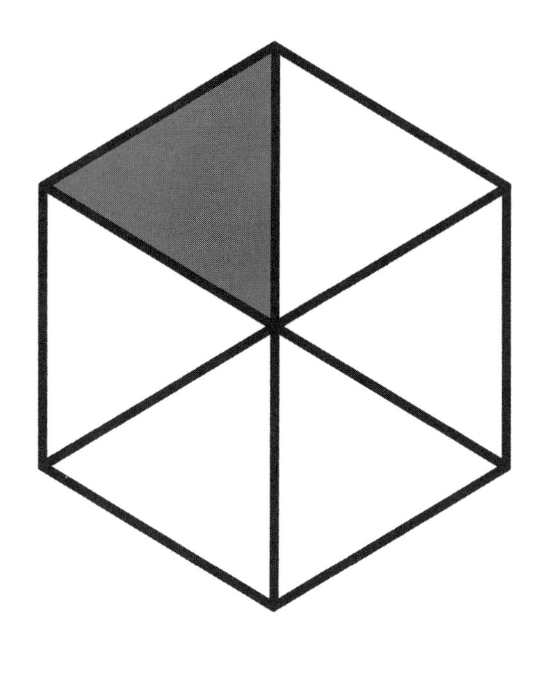

GENEROSITY

Give Back

"You can't live a perfect day without doing something for someone who will never be able to repay you."
John Wooden

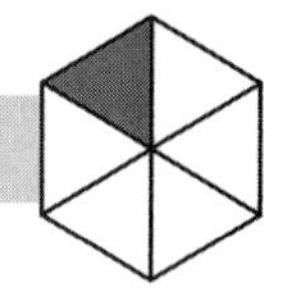

GENEROSITY

"Oh Lord it's hard to be humble."

—Kenny Rogers

HAVING A KEEN SENSE OF HUMILITY IS CONSIDered the toughest of the key principles of *The Wisdom Way*. Being humble in every aspect of your business is the long-term approach to being successful. Humbleness can ultimately serve your bottom line with:

Vendors. Negotiating the lowest price for a given raw material or service at the best delivered cost with high quality and on the best terms is a given. Getting all of this isn't easy. Raking a given vendor over the coals, so to speak, may in the short-term produce the desired result; however, it is cautioned that short-term gains at the cost of long-term issues is not a desirable way to proceed. Having humbleness throughout the lifespan of a relationship with a vendor will allow for upfront negotiations, making your needs clear to the vendor. Humbleness equates with fairness and honesty,

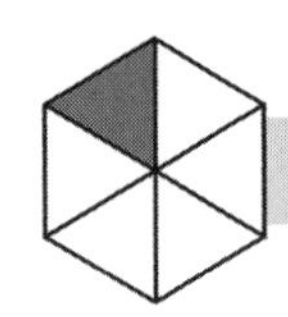

and in the end, all companies worth their salt will not only want to do business with you, but they will raise the standard for all customers they desire to do business with. This is what we call earning our marker with the vendor.

In all the experiences over a lifetime body of work, one key element is clear—at some point, somehow, and in some fashion, you will be called upon to call in your well-earned marker from a vendor to resolve a serious problem that only they can solve.

Case in point, there was a key account in the process of a very lengthy sale of substantial volume, and the necessary commitments from the customer had already been secured and the negotiation of the final drafts of the contract and prequalification already accomplished on the products, when suddenly, a shift in the marketplace required the customer to either meet a new, lower price point or the project would be a bust. The customer communicated what was needed and explained that for the project to move forward, a significant price concession was necessary. This was brought to the attention of a key vendor and service provider on the project, and a marker was called in to make this project ultimately work. The project was critical, most of our resources having been funneled in to make this project work. With it, the year was made; without it, it was unlikely that sales and profitability goals would be met. In the end, the marker was honored and the business was secured. All parties involved, the vendor, Wisdom Adhesives, and the customer, were satisfied with the result. One cannot overstate the significance of the building of a humble relationship with the vendor (and the customer)

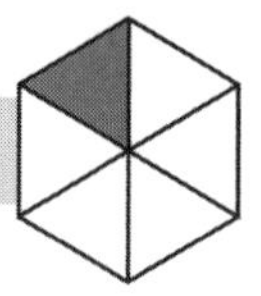

as having been the key component and guiding principle in making the business deal move forward to become successful.

As a post-note to this story, this vendor and this particular customer are strong allies and valued members of the Wisdom Adhesives business community.

Customers. Making a profit requires selling a finished product for more than what it takes to produce it. This is the Simple Simon approach. How much profit and where to get it are key components to any sound business strategy.

Being humble not only in business but in your personal life is important.

"Humbleness is next to Godliness" is very true.

Grandstanding an achievement, like gaining a new account, or overstressing the significance of one individual's importance in a truly team concept can be damaging to the entire team. Celebration is significant. It is important to celebrate the good times and the achievements. Doing so as a team is paramount. Doing so as an individual, claiming to have done it all by one's self, is ultimately damaging to the organization and is like a cancer that will spread to all reaches of the company. It is important to cultivate a culture in the business where humility is looked upon as strength and a desired quality for all employees to embrace. It is equally important for top management to reward humility and reprimand the opposite.

For many organizations it is simply not natural to reward humility. Many look upon a humble person as one who is weak and meek. At Wisdom Adhesives, team play is rewarded with promotions, monetary bonuses, and frank

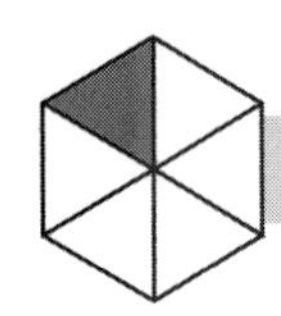

recognition. The meek shall inherit the earth, says the Bible. In *The Wisdom Way*, the meek and humble shall inherit the business.

Generosity can come in many forms and ideas, as shown below:

- Generosity Is the Ultimate Long-Term Strategy
- Rewarding
- Incubation
- Spirituality
- Zen Mastering—The Art of the Sherpa

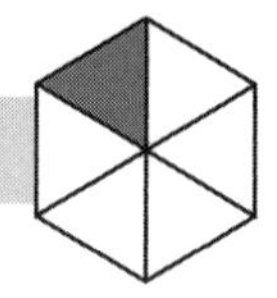

Generosity Is the Ultimate Long-Term Strategy

THERE WAS THIS INVENTOR-TYPE GUY WHO FOR YEARS was thinking of bringing his invention to market. Not because he wanted to make a million bucks on it, but because he wanted to share the fun and the knowledge with those he thought would benefit.

Then Wisdom Adhesives came into his life through unconventional means and helped him realize his dream. They taught him what generosity really means and showed him grace, friendship, kindness, and fun.

This affected him in deep and powerful ways. It gave him comfort to build such a deep and long-lasting friendship.

Generosity pays you back in ways you can't see initially.

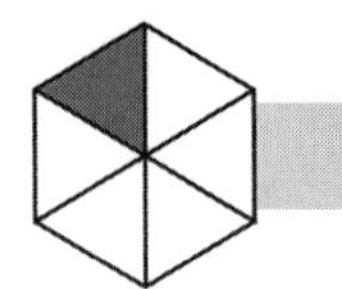

Generosity Is Its Own Reward

Generosity is good business. It is always your best spend. Generosity is not understood by finance alone. It is an intangible. There is no case accrual or trade fund set up for generosity. This is your opportunity to separate yourself from the pack.

Generosity is its own reward. Be Generous with it.

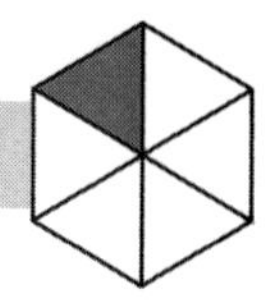

Incubation

INCUBATION. IT'S THE TAKING OF SOMETHING FRESH, IN need of help, and nurturing it to fruition. At Wisdom Adhesives, there is a formal incubator program that takes ideas brought up by personnel at all levels, as well as outside entrepreneurs and funds their start-up costs. An incubator committee screens the applicants, and every year, a few are given the opportunity to move forward. While some have stalled due to a variety of reasons, many ventures have been successful.

Incubation. Generosity. It's *The Wisdom Way*.

Generosity Brings Out Your Spirituality

GENEROSITY BRINGS OUT YOUR SPIRITUALITY. IT IS your inner voice and one that is underdeveloped in the business world. A strong spirit will provide the key qualities of the other five Wisdom Way principles (Passion, Action, Reinvention, Endurance, and Relationships) far better than what is without.

Practicing generosity taps your spirit from within. Your inner voice. Your subconscious. In today's busy world, it's often hard to listen to your soul, your spirit. Generosity brings out the inner workings of a person, making them the best they can possible be.

Increasing Spirituality = Increasing Generosity = Getting More Out of Life and More Out of Business Dealings

Listen to your soul, your spirit. Be Generous.

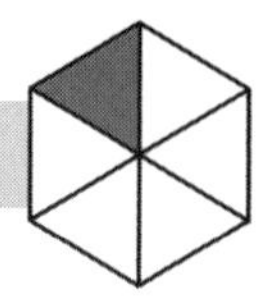

Zen Mastering

ZEN MASTERING IS THE ART OF THE SHERPA. BEING THE leader of a cause, not necessarily for profit, but for profitability. The difference lies in the philosophy of approach.

Generosity isn't always about providing money or time or financial assets. Generosity also means giving your knowledge to those in need of it. A Sherpa in the business world today is the leader by example, leader by knowledge, leader by spirituality. It's the spirituality that separates one organization from the next. Many, many companies are faceless and, most certainly, Sherpa-less. This isn't the case, most fortunately, for Wisdom Adhesives.

Be Generous, be someone's Sherpa.

CHRONOLOGICAL HISTORY

Five Generations

Past Presidents & Chief Executive Officers at Wisdom Adhesives

1ST GENERATION

Phillip Wisdom

2ND GENERATION

George Wisdom

3RD GENERATION

Harry Wisdom

4TH GENERATION

George Wisdom

Carl Wisdom

John Wisdom

5TH GENERATION

Jeff Wisdom

Below is a key milestone chronological history of Wisdom Adhesives:

1875—Phillip Wisdom initializes the business on Canal Street in Chicago, Illinois, erecting a sign—"Wisdom & Company, Western Depot and Glue." Wisdom becomes a manufacturer and seller of industrial adhesives.

1900—Wisdom Adhesives celebrates 25 years in business. Top client is George Pullman & Company, a leading manufacturer of railroad equipment.

1910–1920s—Wisdom Adhesives helps the literary world come to realization with a full line of adhesives for bookbinding applications. George Wisdom takes over the helm at Wisdom Adhesives.

1925—Company sales reach a new milestone.

1935—Harry becomes the third -generation president and majority owner of Wisdom Adhesives.

1945—Wisdom Adhesives moves to a larger operation on the South Side of Chicago, Illinois. Sales ramp up markedly since the company's inception. Product line is expanded to include adhesives for graphic arts and paper converting applications.

1955—Wisdom Adhesives expands to a new location in Franklin Park, Illinois. Modernization of the time period takes place.

1960s—New state-of-the-art mixing equipment is installed; growth continues.

1960s—George Wisdom takes the helm of Wisdom Adhesives and further modernizes sales, accounting, and manufacturing processes. Sales incrementally grow significantly during his tenure.

1970s–1980s—Technology, manufacturing, and sales growth are the order of the day for the '70s and '80s. The 100th anniversary of Wisdom Adhesives is celebrated with a company picnic with the key customers and vendors in attendance. Karl becomes acting president of Wisdom Adhesives.

1980s–1990s—John Wisdom assumes leadership of the company and spurs further growth of capabilities, technologies, and sales.

1990s—Expansion to Los Angeles, California, and Boston, Massachusetts, for warehousing and production. Overseas operations in China, India, and Japan are opened.

1980s–1990s—Sales of bookbinding adhesives continue to expand into Asia and Europe. Development of Wisdom International signals a new era for the company. Significant growth of overseas products and sales are seen just prior to the new millennium.

1990s–2000—Jeff Wisdom—fifth-generation owner—becomes president of Wisdom Adhesives. Product lines are further expanded to packaging and assembled products, in addition to graphic arts and paper converting.

2000s—Expansion to Southeastern United States locations for adhesive production. Annual sales reach new milestones.

2000s—Wisdom Adhesives moves to their new state-of-the-art location in Elgin, Illinois. Capabilities, sales, and technologies all rapidly advance. WizBond Adhesives are leading the way.

2000s—Establishment of the Wisdom Global Adhesives Group—sales in over 13 countries.

2000s—ClearBond hot melt product line introduced. Further technological growth continues. Operations are expanded to Canada and Mexico with the establishment of Wisdom Mexico and Wisdom Canada.

2005—Establishment of several new programs, including WTQM LSS-FAST, ECO^2 Management, GreenBond Sustainable Adhesive Product Line, the WizNet Online Ordering System, and The Wisdom Foundation, and the installation of a hot melt line in Elgin, Illinois. Sales set to surpass record levels.

Operations are expanded to the Caribbean with the establishment of Wisdom Caribbean. New technologies to Wisdom are produced locally.

2008—Sales continue to grow at a rapid pace. Continued expansion into North American and international operations. T3 (Tiger Team) initiated to combat and find alternatives to raw material cost increases and improvement of efficiencies. Newly innovative and environmentally compatible hot melt line of olefin-based products is introduced. GreenBond Sustainable Adhesive Scorecard rolled out.

Wisdom establishes manufacturing and additional warehousing in Western United States.

2011—Wisdom Adhesives is now ***Wisdom Adhesives Worldwide***. The name change reflects Wisdom's rapidly growing importance in supplying premium adhesives to the global packaging and converting markets.

2012–2014—Introduction of WizAssure line of olefin-based hot melt adhesives. Continued expansion in globally and in North American .

2015—Wisdom Adhesives Worldwide celebrates 140 years of existence, maintaining its mark as the longest running adhesive manufacturing company in North America and possibly the world!

THE NEXT 140 YEARS

TOMORROW IS NOT PROMISED TO ANY OF US. THIS is true in life and in business. Even though there are contracts in place, long-time and new customers always seemingly placing orders, it is a fact that no business is totally promised. Contracts can be broken; customers can change suppliers or go out of business. Therefore, it is especially important to stick to one's principles and to forge ahead in good and in bad times.

Wisdom Adhesives was founded on long-term thinking and long-lasting actions and endeavors. If one sticks to the principles of *The Wisdom Way* over an extended period of time, success is not only possible but probable.

- Having PASSION in all facets of the business is the driving force for continuation. It's what drives one to wake up and start the day. Getting the "early W" is important to gain momentum throughout the day.

- The "early W" also sets the tone with ACTION. Do something, move the needle, push forward. All of these ACTIONS are necessary for success. Success begets success, and it all begins with ACTION.

- Lacking REINVENTION is where PASSION and ACTION begin to stall. Continually striving to find methods to do better are key to survival. It has been key to Wisdom Adhesives' survival and the basis for *The Wisdom Way*.

- Having inner strength or ENDURANCE allows one to REINVENT and fuel PASSION into ACTION to drive success, even in the worst of times. ENDURANCE is a quality that cannot be bought; it must be earned, earned from each and every process, task, sale, or the like. ENDURANCE has the power to build long and lasting alliances.

- At some point in everyone's life, career, or business ventures, they can look back and name those people who really helped them through tough times. Anyone can help in good times, but it is in the toughest of times that RELATIONSHIPS are the most valued and the most critical.

- "Pay it forward" is a phrase often used for doing a task that has no or a limited prospect of a return. Having the GENEROSITY to pay it forward generally results in good begetting good. Good things will happen to GENEROUS endeavors.

Looking ahead, Wisdom Adhesives has the PASSION, ACTION, REINVENTION, ENDURANCE, RELATIONSHIPS, and GENEROSITY to thrive for the next generations, the sixth, seventh and eighth generations, and the next 140 years.

GLOSSARY: SIX PRINCIPLES OF THE WISDOM WAY

Passion: Any powerful or compelling emotion or feeling, as love or hate; strong amorous feeling or desire; love; ardor

Action: The process or state of acting or of being active; something done or performed; act; deed

Reinvention: To invent again or anew, especially without knowing that the invention already exists; to remake or make over, as in a different form

Endurance: The fact or power of enduring or bearing pain, hardships, etc.; the ability or strength to continue or last, especially despite fatigue, stress, or other adverse conditions; stamina

Relationships: A connection, association, or involvement; an emotional or other connection between people

Generosity: Readiness or liberality in giving; freedom from meanness or smallness of mind or character; a generous act

Dictionary.com Unabridged. Random House, Inc. 29 Jul. 2014. Dictionary.com. <http://dictionary.reference.com/browse/>

THE WISDOM WAY

Passion
Action
Reinvention
Endurance
Relationships
Generosity

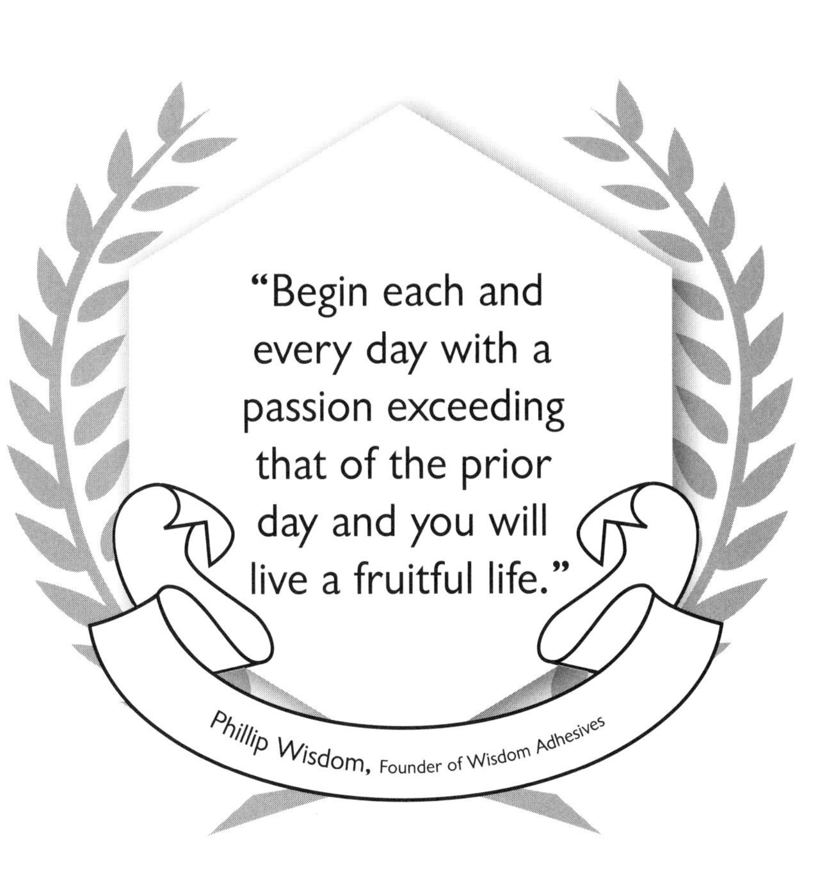
"Begin each and every day with a passion exceeding that of the prior day and you will live a fruitful life."
Phillip Wisdom, Founder of Wisdom Adhesives

"Have passion in your life; it's far too short."
Jeff Wisdom, Wisdom Adhesives 5th Generation Owner

"The Strength of
the Hexagon"

"Don't Be
Afraid to Live"

The Wisdom Way